"I can think of few things that the co[...] much as the ancient practice of lectio di[...] by which we are to receive Scripture. The focus of this series is rightly on the biblical text itself, and the commentary and questions push us back to the text to listen for God's address. My hope is that this well-written and accessible tool will assist readers in the practice of lectio divina."

—Craig Bartholomew, coauthor, *The Drama of Scripture*

"Stephen Binz has done an admirable job of introducing his readers to the process of lectio divina and immersing them in it. Through teaching the practice of this ancient way of studying the Bible, this series of Scripture studies will recharge and deepen the faith and lives of many, who thereafter will use the art for private devotions and/or in small groups. I heartily recommend this series to individuals and churches who want to join in the spirited revival of Christianity in our time!"

—Marva J. Dawn, Regent College

"At their recent Synod the world's Catholic bishops recommended lectio divina to all Christ's disciples, for prayerfully reading and making God's Word one's spiritual nourishment follows well-trod paths in the Christian tradition. Stephen Binz guides us on these paths in his Ancient-Future Bible Study series. I am pleased to recommend this project with enthusiasm."

—Terrence Prendergast, SJ, Archbishop of Ottawa

"Lectio divina, despite its centuries-long use, is still little known outside of monastic and academic settings. Ancient-Future Bible Study, a project that does great credit to Brazos Press, has in mind to correct that historical defect in Christian piety."

—Patrick Henry Reardon, author, *Creation and the Patriarchal Histories*

"Ancient-Future Bible Study brings a centuries-old approach to Scripture and prayer into the twenty-first century, providing sound commentary, thoughtful insights, and meaningful suggestions for personal reflection and meditation. Stephen Binz invites us to open our minds and hearts to the transforming power of God's Word. Under his guidance, the wisdom of the Bible comes vividly to life."

—Carl McColman, author, *The Big Book of Christian Mysticism*

"Stephen Binz has a knack for popularizing the Bible. His latest series, Ancient-Future Bible Study, demonstrates once more his ability to give people sound guidance as they read the Bible. I am happy to warmly recommend this modern application of the ancient method of lectio divina—the once and future way to read the Bible prayerfully—centered on fascinating characters from the Old and New Testaments."

—Fr. Ronald D. Witherup, author, *The Bible Companion*

"A method of Bible study that has a long and celebrated history in the church is given renewed momentum with this series. The goal here is more than instruction. The five movements of lectio divina are an invitation to immerse oneself in the riches of our biblical tradition and to give flesh to that tradition in our daily lives. This series will be a wonderful aid for the development of one's spiritual life."

—Dianne Bergant, CSA, Catholic Theological Union

"This series is a wonderful gift for the church in late modernity. In an era of twittered attention, we have inculcated all sorts of bad reading habits that we then bring to Scripture. The Ancient-Future Bible Study prescribes a counter-formative regimen: the personal and communal practice of lectio divina or 'sacred reading.' For some this will be a strange, new practice; but it will quickly feel as natural as breathing. So find some friends, take up this series, and read anew!"

—James K. A. Smith, Calvin College; author, *Desiring the Kingdom: Worship, Worldview, and Cultural Formation*

"Stephen Binz's new series allows us to put down the commentaries and word studies and let the beautiful poignancy of the text seep into our souls, all with the aid of the Holy Spirit. I heartily recommend it."

—Tony Jones, Solomon's Porch, Minneapolis; author, *The New Christians: Dispatches from the Emergent Frontier*

"Stephen Binz, a responsible biblical scholar and experienced pastor, has undertaken the important project of leading non-professional but committed readers of the Bible into a spiritually enlivening encounter with the biblical text through engagement with some of the fascinating characters who people its pages. Anyone yearning to pray the biblical text will find this series a useful companion."

—Sandra M. Schneiders, Jesuit School of Theology

ANCIENT-FUTURE BIBLE STUDY

WOMEN
OF THE
GOSPELS

Friends and Disciples of Jesus

STEPHEN J. BINZ

Brazos Press

a division of Baker Publishing Group
Grand Rapids, Michigan

© 2011 by Stephen J. Binz

Published by Brazos Press
a division of Baker Publishing Group
P.O. Box 6287, Grand Rapids, MI 49516-6287
www.brazospress.com

Printed in the United States of America

Library of Congress Cataloging-in-Publication Data
Binz, Stephen J., 1955–
   Women of the Gospels : friends and disciples of Jesus / Stephen J. Binz.
      p.   cm. — (Ancient-future Bible study)
    ISBN 978-1-58743-282-8 (pbk.)
    1. Women in the Bible. 2. Bible. N.T. Gospels—Criticism, interpretation, etc. 3. Devotional literature. I. Title.
    BS2445.B56 2011
    226'.083054—dc22   2010028530

Scripture is taken from the New Revised Standard Version of the Bible, copyright © 1989, by the Division of Christian Education of the National Council of the Churches of Christ in the United States of America. Used by permission. All rights reserved.

Some content from "Welcome to Ancient-Future Bible Study" originally appeared in Stephen J. Binz, *Conversing with God in Scripture: A Contemporary Approach to Lectio Divina* (Ijamsville, MD: The Word Among Us Press, 2008).

11 12 13 14 15 16 17   7 6 5 4 3 2 1

Contents

Acknowledgments

For the past several years my work has focused on making connections between ancient practices and contemporary experiences. My speaking, writing, and counseling under the trademark Bridge-Building Opportunities has emphasized the link between past and present, East and West, time-honored tradition and progressive renewal in the fields of biblical theology, Christian spirituality, and personal growth.

When I discovered the mission of Brazos Press, I felt that I had found a new home. By its own definition, Brazos Press is "staked on the discernment that while various existing Christian categories (liberal and conservative, mainline and evangelical, even Catholic and Protestant) prove increasingly unserviceable, there is at the same time occurring a robust renewal of classical, orthodox Christianity across many of the old lines or borders." This is a publisher that is eager to cross boundaries, build bridges, and extend the vital roots of the ancient Christian tradition into the twenty-first century.

I am grateful to Jim Kinney, associate publisher and editorial director of Baker Academic and Brazos Press, for supporting my work. Lisa Ann Cockrel, editor for this series, has masterfully guided these books through the editorial process and improved this work with her many ideas. I also appreciate the skillful work of Lisa Beth Anderson, Rodney Clapp, Steve Ayers, BJ Heyboer, Jeremy Wells, Caitlin Mackenzie, and the whole Brazos team for their efforts to refine and promote this project.

The term "Ancient-Future" seems to perfectly express the bridge between ancient wisdom and future possibilities that I want to create in this series. The term is applied in a number of other spheres to emphasize a blending of tradition and innovation. In the arts, ancient-future music and dance is created through fusing centuries-old traditions with contemporary genres and technology. By learning from the world's great traditions and ancient practices, artists create cross-cultural expressions that are richly profound yet also widely appealing.

I am particularly indebted to the work of the late Robert Webber, many of whose books use the term "Ancient-Future" to express his mission of drawing wisdom from the past and translating those insights into the present and future life of the church, its faith, worship, ministry, and spirituality. In his own words: "My argument is that the era of the early church (AD 100–500), and particularly the second century, contains insights which evangelicals need to recover." This series resonates with his outstanding work and hopefully, in some small way, will honor his memory and continue his vision.

Finally, I am grateful to all my friends and colleagues in the field of biblical studies and to all pastors, lay ministers, and church volunteers who are dedicated to an anciently rooted and forward-looking Christianity. Particularly I want to express my appreciation to my wife Pamela, a professor of music, for the loving support and inspiration she constantly offers to me.

Welcome to Ancient-Future Bible Study

Ancient-Future Bible Study unites contemporary study of the Bible with an experience of the church's most ancient way of reading Scripture, *lectio divina*. By combining the old and the new in a fertile synthesis, this study helps modern people encounter the *sacra pagina*, the inspired text, as God intends it for the church. Through solid historical and literary study and the time-honored practice of lectio divina, the mind and the heart are brought into an experience of God through a careful and prayerful reading of the biblical texts.

As the Word of its divine author, the Bible is not just a literary anthology of ancient texts; it is inspired literature addressed to God's people. God intends the sacred texts to move from our heads to the depths of our hearts and to form us as a new people living in God's reign. Ancient-Future Bible Study guides readers to listen to Scripture within the tradition and scholarship of the church in order to unleash its life-changing potential.

The ancient art of lectio divina is rooted in the Jewish tradition of Jesus, and it was nourished through the desert spirituality of the early centuries, the patristic writers of the ancient church, and the monastic tradition through the ages. In our day, lectio divina is experiencing a worldwide revival as Christians are returning to age-old wisdom to experience the Scriptures in a deeper and more complete way.

As you experience Ancient-Future Bible Study, you will realize how the church's long tradition of biblical study, reflection, prayer, discernment, and contemplative action can enrich your discipleship. You will learn how to dispose yourself to be formed by the Word of God as you join with the array of men and women through the ages whose lives have been transformed by that same living Word.

Reasons for Studying the Bible

Most often people study the Bible for one of three reasons. First, they study for information and knowledge. This usually includes a search for historical facts, doctrinal truths, and moral guidance. Second, they study to find advice for solving a personal need or getting through a life crisis. This usually involves seeking out lists of specific passages that speak to the particular needs of the moment. Third, they study so they can defend their faith and witness to others. This usually consists of choosing selected passages to remember and quote, so they can argue for a particular approach to faith or help lead others toward the truth. While all of these objectives can lead to good results, their accomplishments are always limited and partial.

The most complete reason for studying Scripture is for the purpose of encountering the living God through the sacred text. This divine encounter leads not just to more information and advice but to a deeply rooted transformation of life. The inspired Word evokes a spiritual transformation within the lives of those who allow God's Word to do its true work, urging us to personal growth in Christ and fuller discipleship.

For Scripture to have its deepest effects in us we must approach the text with humility, reverence, and expectation. As we receive its revelation and understand its truth, Scripture has the ability to gradually change our minds and mold our hearts. Unlike any other literature, the words of the Bible can renew our lives when we approach the text as an encounter with its divine author.

The Indwelling of the Holy Spirit

The Bible was written under the inspiration of the Holy Spirit. God's "breathing in," acting in union with the human authors of the texts, makes the Scriptures the Word of the living God. Because God is the primary author of the Bible, we can be assured that the texts have a power that transcends that of any other spiritual reading.

God's inspiration of the biblical books does not refer only to a past reality, to the historical time in which the biblical authors were guided to write the texts. Rather, the work of God's Spirit is an ongoing reality within the inspired books. The sacred texts remain inspired; they are forever permeated with divine breath and are filled now with the Spirit of God.

This understanding of the Spirit's enduring and ongoing presence in the biblical texts is the foundation of lectio divina. Through the Holy Spirit, God addresses his Word to us here and now through the ancient text. Because of the indwelling Spirit, the Word is alive and has the power to transform us. The Word of God is charged with creative power to change and renew us from within.

The Movements of Lectio Divina

Lectio divina (LEK-tsee-oh dih-VEEN-ah) is best translated, though incompletely, as "sacred reading." Its revitalization, like the renewal of other spiritual practices from the early church, is becoming a means of deep spiritual growth for people today. Lectio divina helps us return to the most ancient understanding of the sacredness of the inspired text. The Bible is not like a textbook, used for looking up factual documentation, nor is it like a manual, describing a how-to method for solving problems. Rather, it is a means of forming our life in God and joining us to the story of God's people.

The process of lectio divina appeals not only to our minds but also to our imaginations and feelings. We seek to understand and experience Scripture as a real communication, as God personally addressing us. In practicing lectio divina, we get caught up in the literature and learn to love the text itself; we read it reflectively, lingering over it, and let it reach the depths of our hearts. We let go of our own agenda and expectations, gradually opening ourselves to what God wants us to experience through the sacred page.

There is no single method for the practice of lectio divina. It is not a rigid step-by-step system for encountering God in biblical passages. The spiritual masters of the early church distrusted methods of prayer and spiritual practice that were too rigidly defined, wishing instead to cultivate the freedom necessary to respond to the Spirit's promptings. Lectio divina aims toward a holistic experience of Scripture, incorporating our intellects, feelings, and actions.

Ancient-Future Bible Study incorporates five "movements." Comparable to the movements in a classical work of music, each movement has its own characteristics and can even be practiced independently of the others. There is plenty of room for personal interpretation within the tradition. Individually and together, lectio, meditatio, oratio, contemplatio, and operatio contribute to the full experience of lectio divina.

Pronunciation Guide

Lectio—LEK-tsee-oh
Meditatio—meh-dih-TAH-tsee-oh
Oratio—oh-RAH-tsee-oh
Contemplatio—con-tem-PLAH-tsee-oh
Operatio—oh-peh-RAH-tsee-oh

Lectio—*Reading the Text with a Listening Ear*

Lectio is more than ordinary reading. It might best be described as listening deeply—what St. Benedict in the sixth century described as hearing "with the ear of our heart." This listening requires that we try to receive God's Word with as little prejudgment as possible, as if we were hearing it for the first time. Lectio urges us to create a space within us for the new wisdom and understanding God wants to give us through the sacred page.

Saint Ambrose in the fourth century urged readers to avoid the tendency to read large passages in haste: "We should read not in agitation, but in calm; not hurriedly, but slowly, a few words at a time, pausing in attentive reflection. . . . Then the readers will experience their ability to enkindle the ardor of prayer." We might even consider returning to the ancient practice of reading texts aloud in order to instill within ourselves the sense of reading Scripture as a deep listening.

The essential question to ask in this first movement is, "What does the text say and what does it mean?" The Jewish rabbis and the church's patristic writers show us that there is no clear distinction between studying and praying Scripture. The more we come to understand the text with our minds, the more we are capable of being changed by the text. Wrestling with the text and seeking to comprehend its meaning is an important part of encountering God there and being changed by that encounter.

Once we've read the text slowly and carefully, Ancient-Future Bible Study invites us to learn from the commentary that follows the biblical passage. This too is part of listening to the text, only here we listen with the understanding of the church and with some basic insights of biblical scholarship. This listening to the text, with its multiple layers of meaning and rich history of interpretation, forms the foundation on which we experience the subsequent movements of lectio divina. We do what we can to make sure our reading of the text is faithful and true, so that we don't reduce God's revelation to our own imaginary constructions. On this firm basis, we construct the process of prayerfully encountering God's Word.

We might read the text as literature, looking at its words, metaphors, images, and characters. We could look at its structure and its literary form—is it poetry, parable, history, proverb, legal code, epic, or apocalypse? We should realize that God's truth is expressed in a variety of types of literature, each type expressing truth in a different way. The more we can comprehend something of the original historical, cultural, literary, and religious context of the passage, the better we will be able to probe all the potential the text can offer us.

In lectio, the words of Scripture become the means of God speaking to us. As God's Spirit guided the human authors to express the truth that God wished to entrust to the Scriptures, God also guides us through that same Spirit as we read the Bible as God's Word to us.

Meditatio—*Reflecting on the Meaning and Message of the Text*

The question to ask in this movement is, "What does the text say to me and mean to me?" Meditatio aims to bring the biblical passage into the sphere of my own life as I seek to understand how the Scripture passage speaks to me today.

Though there is a wide gap of time, language, and culture between the world of the biblical writers and our own world, meditatio bridges that gap. By reflecting on the text as well as on our own experiences, thoughts, challenges, and questions, we can grow in our understanding that God is speaking personally to us through the scriptural text. This reflection forms connections between the text of yesterday and the today of our lives.

Ancient-Future Bible Study stimulates meditatio through the use of questions for reflection. These questions encourage a deeper and more personal consideration of the text. They challenge the reader to create a dialogue between the ancient text and life today. As the Word of God, the Bible has a richness of meaning that can be discovered in every age and every culture. It has a particular message that can be received by everyone who listens to God's Word in the context of daily experiences and in the same Spirit in which it was written.

The more we meditate on God's Word, the more it seeps into our lives and saturates our thoughts and feelings. Meditatio allows the dynamic Word of God to so penetrate our lives that it truly infuses our minds and hearts and we begin to embody its truth and its goodness.

Oratio—*Praying in Response to God's Word*

Careful lectio and reflective meditatio open the way for God to enter into our hearts and inflame them with the grace of his love. There, at the core of our being, we naturally want to respond to the One whose voice we have heard. Oratio is our prayerful response to God's Word.

Lectio divina is fundamentally a dialogue with God, a gentle oscillation between listening to God and responding to him in prayer. When we recognize that God has offered us a message that is unique to our own lives—an insight, a challenge, a comfort, a call—we arrive at the moment when we must ask ourselves, "Now what am I going to say in response to God?" This is the moment of prayer.

Oratio is not just any form of prayer. It is born from the experience of listening to God in Scripture. The biblical words we have heard and reflected on become the words of our prayer. The style and vocabulary of our prayer are enriched through the inspired words of the biblical tradition. Whether our oratio is an act of praise or thanksgiving, of petition or repentance, we pray in response to what we have heard. Our prayers no longer consist of mechanically repeated formulas. Rather, they resonate with the faith, hope, and love that animated the people of the Bible in their journey with God.

Ancient-Future Bible Study offers examples of this type of prayer. After each session of lectio and meditatio, we are encouraged to continue in intimate prayer to God, melding the words, images, and sentiments of the biblical text with personal thoughts, feelings, and desires arising from the heart.

Contemplatio—*Quietly Resting in God*

Both oratio and contemplatio are forms of prayer. Oratio is our active, word-filled prayer in response to God's Word. Contemplatio is prayer without words. It is the response to God that remains after words are no longer necessary or helpful. It is simply enjoying the experience of quietly being in God's presence.

Contemplatio requires that we let go of any effort to be in charge of the process. When we feel God drawing us into a deeper awareness of his divine presence, we gradually abandon our intellectual activity and let ourselves be wooed into God's embrace. We no longer have to think or reason, listen or speak. The experience resembles that of lovers holding each other in wordless silence or of a sleeping child resting in the arms of his or her mother.

Though we may think the movement of contemplatio is passive and uneventful, it is not. When we humbly expose our heart, the center of our being, to God, what happens within us during those moments is really not up to us. In contrast to the rapid, noisy communication of our technological world, quiet, receptive stillness is the atmosphere in which the most important communication occurs. God's grace is truly at work in those moments, and the Holy Spirit is changing us without our direct knowledge or understanding.

Operatio—*Faithful Witness in Daily Life*

After reading, reflecting, and praying over a scriptural passage, we should be impacted in a way that makes a difference in our daily lives. Operatio is our lived response to the biblical text. The question operatio calls forth from us is, "How can I live out the Word of God that I have heard in my heart?"

We cannot prayerfully read Scripture without being changed in some specific way. As we deepen our relationship with God through the movements of lectio divina, our actions become vehicles of his presence to others. We become channels of God's compassion and mercy, becoming "doers of the word, and not merely hearers" (James 1:22), bringing about God's loving purposes in our daily lives.

Contemplatio and operatio should not be totally distinct and separate. Their impulses grow together in the heart of one who prayerfully reads Scripture. Contemplatio does not separate us from the world, and operatio is not genuine unless it grows out of contemplative reflection. Apart from contemplatio, operatio could become superficial pragmatism.

The Bible should never be viewed as simply a collection of maxims to be put into practice. Rarely does Scripture offer us concrete details about what to do in specific situations. Our human reason and experience must always accompany our prayerful discernment as we decide how to live out the Word of God. Listening, reflection, prayer, and contemplation are all necessary components from which flows the operatio of Christian discipleship. Lectio divina helps us become contemplative activists and active contemplatives.

The Essence of Lectio Divina

The movements of lectio divina are more like the colors of a rainbow than clearly defined stages. They overlap, blending into one another, ebbing and flowing according to the rhythm of the divine Spirit and the human heart. The five movements used in Ancient-Future Bible Study are part of a rich tradition, though additional phases are sometimes found in other historical forms of the practice: studium (study), cogitatio (reflection), consolatio (comfort), discretio (discernment), deliberatio (decision making), compassio (compassion), and actio (action).

While the most ancient practice of lectio divina is not a rigid system of biblical reflection, nor does its method require any particular steps, there are a few characteristics that identify the authentic practice of lectio divina:

✝ *Lectio divina is a personal encounter with God through Scripture.* The text itself is a gateway to God. Through the inspired Scripture, we meet the God who loves us and desires our response.

✝ *Lectio divina establishes a dialogue between the reader of Scripture and God.* The attentive reader listens to God through the text and responds to God in heartfelt prayer. The heart of lectio divina is this gentle conversation with God.

✝ *Lectio divina creates a heart-to-heart intimacy with God.* In the Bible, the heart is a person's innermost core, the place from which one's deepest longings, motivations, decisions, memories, and desires arise. The prayerful reader responds to God's Word with the whole heart and thereby grows in a relationship with God at the deepest level of intimacy.

✝ *Lectio divina leads to contemplation and action.* There is a moment in all true love that leads to a level of communication too deep for words. Prayerful reading inevitably leads to that deepest form of communication with God, which is loving silence. In addition, all true love must be expressed in action. Eventually words become inadequate, and love must be demonstrated in deeds arising from a changed heart.

The Word of God and its power to change us are gifts from God that we must accept into our lives. In order to receive the gift of divine intimacy, we must create the necessary conditions within us. Openheartedness, faithfulness, and expectation will enable us to more readily listen and receive. The more we remove the obstacles in the way—our inner resistance, our fear of intimacy, our impatient awareness of time, our desire to control the process, and our self-concern—the more we can expect Scripture to transform our lives.

Sometimes the changes are remarkable; more often they are subtle. We gradually become aware that the fruit of studying the Bible is the fruit of the Spirit: "love, joy, peace, patience, kindness, generosity, faithfulness, gentleness, and self-control" (Gal. 5:22–23). When we begin to notice this fruit in the way we live each day, we will know that the Word of God is working within us.

Your Personal Practice of Ancient-Future Bible Study

✝ This study is designed to provide maximum flexibility so that you can make lectio divina a regular part of your life according to your circumstances. If you are able to make the time in your daily schedule, you will want to reflect on one chapter each day. If not, you may select three weekdays to read three chapters per week. Or if your weekends are more leisurely, you may choose to reflect on two chapters per weekend.

‡ Reading Plan #1—30 days/5 weeks
  • Engage six lessons per week

‡ Reading Plan #2—60 days/10 weeks
  • Engage three lessons per week

‡ Reading Plan #3—90 days/15 weeks
  • Engage two lessons per weekend

‡ Whatever pace you choose for your practice of lectio divina, try to find a regular time during the day that can become a pattern for you. Choose a quiet and comfortable place where you will be undisturbed during the time of your lectio divina.

‡ During your regular time for lectio divina, try to rid yourself of as many distractions as possible. Before you begin reading the Bible, take time to call upon the Holy Spirit for guidance. Light a candle, ring a chime, kiss the Bible, or do some other action that will designate these moments as sacred time.

‡ Read the biblical text slowly and carefully. Read the passage in another translation, if you wish, to help your understanding. Don't hesitate to mark up this book with highlights, underlining, circles, or whatever will help you pay attention and remember the text and commentary.

‡ Follow the movements of lectio divina outlined in each section. Realize that this is only a tentative guide for the more important movements of God's Spirit within you. Write out your responses to the questions provided. The questions following the lectio are objective questions synthesizing your reading of the text and commentary. Those under meditatio are more personal questions, requiring thoughtful reflection. Try also to write comments on the sections of oratio, contemplatio, and operatio, according to the suggestions provided. The very act of writ-

ing will help you clarify your thoughts, bring new insights, and amplify your understanding.

‡ Approach your lectio divina with expectancy, trusting that God will indeed work deeply within you through his Word. Through this experience, know that you are placing yourself within a long procession of God's people through the ages who have allowed themselves to be transformed through lectio divina.

‡ Finally, try to be accountable to at least one other person for your regular practice of lectio divina. Tell a spouse, friend, spiritual director, or minister about your experience in order to receive their encouragement and affirmation.

Bringing Ancient-Future Bible Study to Churches

Throughout the history of salvation, God's Word has been directed first and foremost to a community, not just to individuals. The people of Israel, the community of disciples, and the early church were the recipients of God's self-communication expressed in the Scriptures. For this reason, studying the Bible in the context of a community of faith can deepen and enrich our individual experience.

Churches and other faith communities may choose to adopt Ancient-Future Bible Study and encourage its use in a variety of ways. Since this Bible study is ideally suited both for personal use by individuals and for communal practice, congregations are able to respect the many ways people desire to make Scripture a priority in their lives. By encouraging an array of options for participation, churches will increase the number of people in the congregation who are making reading and reflection on the Bible a regular part of their lives in Christ.

Collatio—The Communal Practice of Lectio Divina

The ancient term for the communal practice of lectio divina is collatio (coh-LAH-tsee-oh), a term that originally meant "a bringing together, interchange, or discussion." Its aim is building up a spiritual community around the Word of God. Collatio began in an age when books were rare and precious. Today, when everyone may have their own Bible, collatio may be practiced in many different ways.

Here are some ways of building up a faith community with Ancient-Future Bible Study:

‡ Offer this study to people who want to participate only on their own. Respect the fact that many people don't have the time or desire to gather with others. Instead they can be encouraged to read and reflect on their own with the prayerful support of the whole community.

‡ Promote the formation of informal groups made up of family, friends, neighbors, or work associates.

‡ Facilitate usage of the study through online communities or social networks. Online group members might want to commit themselves to sending an email or text message to the group offering their insights after reflecting on each Scripture passage.

‡ Set up small groups that meet regularly at church facilities or in homes. These groups may meet at different times throughout the week to offer convenient options for people in different circumstances. Groups could be made up of people with obvious connections: young adults, retired seniors, parents with young children, professionals, couples, etc. These groupings may encourage a deeper level of personal reflection among members.

Biblical reading and reflection on a regular basis is an important part of Christian discipleship. Every member of our congregations should be encouraged to make Bible reading and reflection a regular part of their lives. This is best accomplished when pastoral leadership promotes this practice and when people are personally invited to participate. When practicing lectio divina within a community of faith, we learn to place our own lives into the story of God's people throughout the ages.

Further Help for Groups

‡ Additional information for facilitating small groups with Ancient-Future Bible Study may be found starting on page 163 of this book.

‡ Since Ancient-Future Bible Study is divided into units of six lessons, motivated groups may choose to study five lessons per week on their own, with a weekly group session discussing insights from the daily lessons and practicing the sixth lesson of the week in the group.

‡ Groups with less daily time to study may divide the six lessons in half, choosing to study two lessons per week on their own, with a weekly group session discussing insights from the daily lessons and practicing the third lesson of the week in the group.

‡ The practice of lectio divina for each lesson will take about thirty minutes for an individual. Those who wish to spend extended time in reflection and prayer should allow for more time. The group session, using the suggestions at the back of this book, will take about ninety minutes.

‡ Additional information about Ancient-Future Bible Study, with descriptions of published and upcoming studies, may be found online at www .brazospress.com/ancientfuturebiblestudy. You can also connect to the series and author on Facebook.

Introduction to *Women of the Gospels: Friends and Disciples of Jesus*

By listening closely to the Gospel narratives, we can appreciate the extraordinarily positive relationships Jesus had with women. When set in the social context of the first-century Jewish culture in which Jesus lived, his understanding of the roles of women is quite revolutionary. Before the ministry of Jesus it was unheard of for women to be disciples of a great teacher, much less to travel with that teacher and participate in his ministry.

Not only did Jesus accept women as disciples, but he also considered women the equal of men as beneficiaries of God's blessings and in the responsibilities that come with God's grace. The Gospels often portray Jesus teaching women and using their lives as models of true discipleship. In the account of Martha and Mary, Jesus is shown to prefer for a woman to listen and learn from him rather than to serve him in the traditional domestic capacity of women. Jesus is shown instructing women as well as men and entering into theological discussions with them, such as he demonstrates with the Samaritan woman at the well. Jesus's treatment of women is consistently ennobling and affectionate, as shown with the woman who anointed Jesus and the widow in the temple who gave her all.

The women Jesus encountered in the Gospel narratives were mothers, wives, daughters, sisters, single women, and widows. Some were influential and wealthy; others were dispossessed and destitute. Most shared the Jewish culture of Jesus; a few were from outside the covenant community. Though it was the social and religious norm of the time that people marry and bear children, Jesus traveled with people who were both married and single. He supported people's desire to remain single and praised the choice based on their motivation—"for the sake of the kingdom of heaven" (Matt. 19:12). Many widows who became disciples chose to live together and devote themselves to ministry rather than remarry. Though family was important for Jesus, among his disciples the family of faith superseded the biological family as the primary bond (Mark 3:35). This new understanding of women in the life and teachings of Jesus had a liberating effect on women, and they responded with deep gratitude and loyalty as his disciples.

The evangelists invite us to get to know these women of the Gospels. When we read their stories, we find that we have much in common with them. Their lives are filled with daily tasks and countless cares. They are women of flesh and blood, with faults and virtues. We see their impatience, jealousies, and frustrations—their desires, passions, and heartaches. Yet overall, we witness their strength, faithfulness, courage, obedience, tenderness, patience, and compassion. These are heroes of faith we can admire and women we can hold up as models for our own lives.

Questions to Consider

✝ What was it about Jesus that made him so attractive to so many women? In what ways does that attraction continue today?

✝ What do I hope to understand and gain from this study of women in the Gospels?

Women Named and Unnamed in the Gospels

Throughout the Gospels, many women and men remain unnamed, identified only by their role or condition—the paralytic man, the Canaanite women, the rich young man, the poor widow. Yet in the four Gospels, fifteen women are identified by their given names. Three of these are women from the Hebrew Scriptures included in the genealogy of Jesus: Tamar, Rahab, and Ruth. Another is the princess Herodias, the wife of Herod. Three others appear in Jesus's infancy account: Elizabeth, the mother of John the Baptist; Mary, the mother of Jesus; and Anna the prophet. The remaining eight named women are disciples of Jesus: Mary Magdalene; Martha and Mary of Bethany; Joanna; Susanna; Mary, the mother of James and Joses; Mary, the wife of Clopas; and Salome.

Many women, as was customary in the first-century culture, are identified by reference to their husband, father, or sons, like Peter's mother-in-law, Jairus's daughter, and the mother of Zebedee's sons. Yet, it does not appear that the names of women were systematically eliminated from the Gospel texts. Rather, it seems that the names of both men and women were retained in the Gospel traditions only when the named persons were recognized figures within the early Christian communities. This is the case with nine women—the eight named disciples and Mary, the mother of Jesus—and about twenty-four men. For this reason, there are more named men than women, but the fact that over one-third are women is a uniquely remarkable occurrence in the culture of the times.

Because names are so important for personal relationships, we wish we knew the names of the many women whose stories have an undeniable impact on the way we understand our Christian faith and live our discipleship. We wish we knew the name of the woman who reached out from the crowd to touch the garment of Jesus or the name of the widow of Nain who mourned her only son. We wonder what name Jesus used to address the woman at the well or the bent-over women who stood up straight after he laid his hands on her. Wouldn't we love to know the name of the bride at whose wedding Jesus produced abundant wine or that anonymous woman who bathed the feet of Jesus with her tears?

Jesus called forth those who were invisible to the political and religious authorities of his day, and they were seen. He spoke with those who had no voice, and they were heard. Jesus touched those who were oppressed by evil systems and immobilized by infirmity, and their lives were brought to wholeness. Forgiven and liberated, strengthened and empowered, women who once felt nameless and worthless followed Jesus and were given courage and eternal purpose.

‡ What does it feel like to be recognized and called by name? Why is it so critical that fellow disciples know my name and understand my story?

‡ Who are the women in my life who have been models and inspirations to me?

2nd Session Intro

One Jesus, Four Gospels, and Many Women

The first page of the New Testament, the opening genealogy of Matthew's Gospel, includes four women from the Old Testament leading to "Mary, of whom Jesus was born." These four women of Israel's covenant remind us that the long history of salvation before Jesus is filled with matriarchs, female heroes, prophets, and wisdom figures. The infancy narrative of Luke's Gospel presents three unlikely women—a barren wife, a young maiden, and an elderly widow. These stories of Elizabeth, Mary, and Anna glow with anticipation of the life of Jesus and present us with models of patience, trust, and devotion.

Mark's Gospel was written in a community suffering persecution under Nero. The women of this Gospel demonstrate faithful discipleship under threat. Their stories offer examples of Jesus's healing touch in situations of suffering and the salvation brought with the coming of God's reign. Matthew's Gospel uses Mark's Gospel as its source and adapts the stories of women in ways that address the needs of a community of Jews and Gentiles facing confrontation and conflict.

Luke's Gospel addresses a community of Gentiles with increasing diversity among its people. It contains several stories of women that are not contained in the other Gospels. There is a clear desire by the author to pair stories about men with stories about women to demonstrate that man and woman stand together, side by side, in the new community founded in Jesus. This plan is extended into Luke's second volume, Acts of the Apostles, which demonstrates that women are prophets, teachers, leaders of house churches, and coworkers in ministry alongside men in the new churches.

The fourth Gospel features women in several episodes unique to this Gospel. The mother of Jesus, the Samaritan woman, Mary and Martha, and Mary Magdalene are all positive portrayals of how women responded to Jesus. These accounts show women progressing in understanding and faith in Jesus as they learn to follow him. Because the role of women in the Christian community was hotly debated as John's Gospel was written, the Gospel writer wanted to present women as models of the process of becoming disciples and bearing witness to the faith.

Finally, it is in the passion and resurrection accounts of each Gospel that the heroism of women truly shines. The poor widow who gives her whole livelihood becomes a prototype of the total self-offering of Jesus, while the woman at Bethany prophetically anoints his body for burial with her perfumed oils. The women who followed Jesus from his early ministry in Galilee continue to follow, and they remain with him at the cross as loyal disciples and witnesses of the crucifixion. These same women accompany his corpse to the tomb and honor his body even in death. Because of such faithfulness to the end, they are also the first witnesses to his resurrection. The evangelists demonstrate in their Gospel accounts that these women were often better models of faithful discipleship than Jesus's chosen twelve.

Questions to Consider

‡ Why would the Gospel writers want to highlight for their Christian communities the stories of women disciples?

✠ The beginning and the end of the Gospel story emphasize the role of individual women. Why would the evangelists want to spotlight women especially at the birth and the death of Jesus?

Learning from the Women of the Gospels

We are increasingly realizing today that the activity of women in the ministry of Jesus was far more crucial and vital than previously recognized or admitted. The stories of women that were remembered, preserved, and eventually canonized in the Gospels are those that reveal what was most valued and cherished in the early Christian community. As the church continually rereads these Gospel narratives in every age, the truths and insights that can be derived from them gradually unfold as people study them in the context of their own lives.

As we begin to imaginatively enter these Gospel accounts of women through the inspired Scriptures, our practice of lectio divina can help us hold the images of these women close to our minds and hearts. Attentive listening, meditating, and praying with these texts will allow us to embrace their stories and bring these women into our own journey of life with Jesus. They will become sources of wisdom for us as we learn from them about courage, holiness, commitment, discernment, and service.

In our meditatio we should always consider ways in which the stories of these biblical women are similar to our own. By seeking these parallels, we can realize that the way God worked in their lives can inform us about the ways that God works in our own lives. These women, often courageous in their suffering and challenged beyond hope, found revitalization and hope because Jesus entered and transformed their lives.

Our task as disciples is, first, to receive the loving attention and encouragement Jesus wants to give us no matter how nameless, dishonored, or powerless we may feel. Then we must extend the saving call of Jesus to others who may feel invisible and voiceless. The community of disciples today continues to be summoned by Jesus to make visible the lives of those who feel out of sight and out of mind, to listen to those whose voice has been silenced by unjust systems, and to touch and empower the lives of those who are downtrodden by forces beyond their control. As disciples of Jesus, we can be instruments of his reign wherever we find ourselves.

Questions to Consider

✢ Why are the stories of women in the Gospels being reexamined and appreciated anew in our day? What is the value of this reassessment?

✢ How can the practice of lectio divina help us to better appreciate and personalize these texts of women in the Gospels?

A Forgotten Advocate for Jesus

Lectio

Carefully read these words from Matthew's Gospel, asking God's Spirit to open your heart.

MATTHEW 27:15–19

¹⁵Now at the festival the governor was accustomed to release a prisoner for the crowd, anyone whom they wanted. ¹⁶At that time

they had a notorious prisoner, called Jesus Barabbas. [17]So after they had gathered, Pilate said to them, "Whom do you want me to release for you, Jesus Barabbas or Jesus who is called the Messiah?" [18]For he realized that it was out of jealousy that they had handed him over. [19]While he was sitting on the judgment seat, his wife sent word to him, "Have nothing to do with that innocent man, for today I have suffered a great deal because of a dream about him."

Continue seeking the significance of this passage for Matthew's passion account.

Pilate's wife is another of those unnamed women of the Gospel accounts who plays a behind-the-scenes role in relationship to an influential man. She intervenes with her powerful husband to try to stop the condemnation of Jesus, an "innocent man." She doesn't even appear in the scene at Pilate's judgment hall; her voice is heard only through a messenger. Only this single verse of Scripture mentions her, so we have no indication whether she had even seen Jesus or encountered him during his ministry in Jerusalem.

The Gospel of Matthew sets up a dramatic contrast between the religious leaders who plead for Jesus Barabbas and Pilate's wife, who pleads for Jesus the Messiah. The leaders are motivated by "jealousy," while Pilate's wife seeks justice for Jesus because of the truth revealed to her in a dream. Both the Jews and Romans took dreams very seriously, and Matthew's account of Jesus's birth had already shown how the Gentile magi received God's warning in a dream in order to save the newborn's life (2:12). Now, in this account of Jesus's death, this Gentile woman intercedes to try to save the life of the Jewish Messiah.

Her pleading is ultimately unsuccessful as her vacillating husband gives in to the pressure of the crowds. The Gospel doesn't tell us what happened to Pilate's wife, either immediately after the crucifixion of Jesus when she encountered her husband again, or the direction of her life from then on. However, the indication that she "suffered a great deal" for Jesus, a New Testament indicator of discipleship, may hint at the later tradition that she became a follower of Christ.

Meditatio

Imagine and consider the behind-the-scenes drama taking place in the heart of Pilate's wife while her husband sits on the judgment seat.

✢ What might be some of the motivations of Pilate's wife in urging her husband to have nothing to do with the murder of this innocent man? What does it tell me about the importance of suffering for the truth?

✢ After the death of Jesus "suffered under Pontius Pilate," what might be some of the conversation between Pilate and his wife? What can I learn and imitate from her witness?

Oratio

Respond in prayer to God, who gives you new insights and hope through listening to his Word.

God of all creation, you created man and woman in your image and sent Jesus the Christ to teach us how to live together in your love. Jesus drew forth the courage and beauty of the women of the Gospels and brought restoration and hope to their lives. He wept with them in their pains, laughed with them in their joys, affirmed them in their resiliency, and empowered their lives with confident trust. Bless my life as I listen, reflect, and pray with the Gospel texts of these women. Transform my life as you did theirs with the power of your Word.

Continue to pray to God from your heart . . .

Contemplatio

Remain in peaceful quiet and place yourself in God's loving embrace. Ask God to give you whatever gift he desires for you during these moments.

Operatio

How can I best dedicate myself to the reflective study of these sacred texts of the Gospels over the coming weeks? What regular place and time could I choose for the quiet practice of lectio divina?

1

Women of Jesus's Genealogy

Lectio

Close off the distractions of the day and enter a still moment where you can listen to the scriptural text with focused attention.

MATTHEW 1:1–16

¹An account of the genealogy of Jesus the Messiah, the son of David, the son of Abraham.

²Abraham was the father of Isaac, and Isaac the father of Jacob, and Jacob the father of Judah and his brothers, ³and Judah the father of Perez and Zerah by Tamar, and Perez the father of Hezron, and Hezron the father of Aram, ⁴and Aram the father of Aminadab, and Aminadab the father of Nahshon, and Nahshon the father of Salmon, ⁵and Salmon the father of Boaz by Rahab, and Boaz the father of Obed by Ruth, and Obed the father of Jesse, ⁶and Jesse the father of King David.

And David was the father of Solomon by the wife of Uriah, ⁷and Solomon the father of Rehoboam, and Rehoboam the father of Abijah, and Abijah the father of Asaph, ⁸and Asaph the father of Jehoshaphat, and Jehoshaphat the father of Joram, and Joram the father of Uzziah, [9]and Uzziah the father of Jotham, and Jotham the father of Ahaz, and Ahaz the father of Hezekiah, [10]and Hezekiah the father of Manasseh, and Manasseh the father of Amos, and Amos the father of Josiah, [11]and Josiah the father of Jechoniah and his brothers, at the time of the deportation to Babylon.

[12]And after the deportation to Babylon: Jechoniah was the father of Salathiel, and Salathiel the father of Zerubbabel, [13]and Zerubbabel the father of Abiud, and Abiud the father of Eliakim, and Eliakim the father of Azor, [14]and Azor the father of Zadok, and Zadok the father of Achim, and Achim the father of Eliud, [15]and Eliud the father of Eleazar, and Eleazar the father of Matthan, and Matthan the father of Jacob, [16]and Jacob the father of Joseph the husband of Mary, of whom Jesus was born, who is called the Messiah.

Search for the significance of this genealogy by exploring the church's scholarship and tradition.

Matthew chooses to begin his Gospel, and thus the New Testament, with a genealogy. Though modern readers sometimes cringe when the genealogies appear in the Bible, ancient peoples considered them important ways of expressing a person's identity. By tracing the Israelite lineage of Jesus, the evangelist demonstrates that Jesus is "the Messiah, the son of David, the son of Abraham" (v. 1). To Abraham, God said, "By your offspring shall all the nations of the earth gain blessing" (Gen. 22:18). To David, God said, "I will establish your descendants forever, and build your throne for all generations" (Ps. 89:4). Israel's prophets expected the Messiah to come from David's royal lineage and establish his everlasting reign.

The genealogy of Jesus reads as expected from one male fathering another until we reach the unexpected inclusion of five women. Their surprising insertion into this masculine league indicates that each of them played a crucial role in God's saving plan to bring Israel to its messianic fulfillment. Yet, these women are not the great matriarchs and female prophets in Israel's history. They seem unlikely choices to be included in the messianic lineage.

Tamar (v. 3), a Canaanite, was left childless after the death of her spouses. She disguised herself as a prostitute and seduced her father-in-law Judah in order to bear a child. Rahab (v. 5), another Canaanite, was a genuine prostitute who sheltered the spies of Israel when they came to Jericho. Ruth, a Moabite, journeyed to Judah after the death of her Israelite husband and married Boaz in Bethlehem. Bathsheba, "the wife of Uriah" (v. 6), a Hittite, became a wife of King David after he shamefully impregnated her and arranged her husband's death.

Each of these women was considered an outsider, a foreigner. Their presence in the genealogy of Jesus foreshadowed the messianic mission, which invited Gentiles as well as Jews into the kingdom of God. Each also had an unusual marital or sexual history that could be seen as scandalous or scornful. Their inclusion along with many corrupt and scandalous men in the genealogy prepares the reader for the ministry of Jesus in which sinners and prostitutes enter the kingdom. Indeed, the universal gospel of Jesus Christ breaks down the barriers between Jew and Gentile, male and female, sinner and saint.

Mary (v. 16) is the final woman in the genealogy. Like the women who preceded her, her marital situation was highly unusual and shocking to outsiders. All five of these women, despite their situations, played an important role in God's providential plan to continue the lineage of the Messiah. Tamar continued the family line of Judah's son. Rahab made it possible for the Israelites to possess the Promised Land. Ruth gave birth to the grandfather of King David. Bathsheba guaranteed that her son Solomon succeeded David. Mary's response to God's unanticipated call enabled her to become God's greatest instrument and to bring the lineage of the Messiah to its completion. The women and men of the genealogy give us a preview of that peculiar collection of humble, marginalized, shameful, and scandalous people who will encounter Jesus and experience the salvation of his kingdom.

The names of Joseph, Mary, and Jesus break the steady rhythm of the genealogical pattern. The shift indicates that Joseph did not father Jesus, according to human descent, and emphasizes that Jesus was born of Mary. The virginal conception of Jesus introduces something radically new as the messianic age dawns. Though adopted by Joseph into David's royal line, Jesus is begotten of God and begins the new era of God's saving plan.

Meditatio

Try to find ways to personalize this text, realizing that all Scripture is inspired and able to teach God's truth. These questions will help apply the text to the context of your life.

‡ Which of my ancestors helped shape my identity? How have they assisted me in my evolving self-understanding?

‡ Who are some of the other great women of Israel whom Jesus would have identified as his ancestors? In what way are these women also my spiritual forebears?

‡ What meaning do I find for myself in Matthew's inclusion of these women in Jesus's genealogy?

Oratio

Pray to God from your heart in whatever way seems to respond to the divine Word spoken to you in the Scriptures. You may use this prayer as a launching pad to continue in your own words.

God of the covenant, you inspired your evangelist Matthew to introduce the Good News of Christ through recalling your relationship with ancient Israel. Help me to recognize that the men and women of the old covenant are the holy ancestors of Jesus and the source of his Jewish faith. Give me an appreciation of your ancient covenant so that I may live abundantly in the new covenant.

Continue to pray to God from your heart . . .

Contemplatio

Imagine your spiritual and familial ancestors gathered around you, praying for you and encouraging you. Relax in this supportive image and trust in the goodness of those who have traveled the path of life before you.

After a period of quiet trust, write a few words about your experience.

Operatio

What characteristics of my biblical or personal ancestors do I most admire? What of their spirit would I like to incorporate into my life?

2

Mary Brings Forth
the Savior to the World

Lectio

Light a candle, ring a chime, or kiss the page of Scripture as you create a sacred space around you and sanctify this time of lectio.

MATTHEW 1:18–25

[18]Now the birth of Jesus the Messiah took place in this way. When his mother Mary had been engaged to Joseph, but before they lived together, she was found to be with child from the Holy Spirit. [19]Her husband Joseph, being a righteous man and unwilling to expose her to public disgrace, planned to dismiss her quietly. [20]But just when he had resolved to do this, an angel of the Lord appeared to him in a dream and said, "Joseph, son of David, do not be afraid to take Mary as your wife, for the child conceived in her is from the Holy Spirit. [21]She will bear a son, and you are to name him Jesus, for he will save his people from their sins."

[22]All this took place to fulfill what had been spoken by the Lord through the prophet: [23]"Look, the virgin shall conceive and bear a son, and they shall name him Emmanuel," which means, "God is with us."

²⁴When Joseph awoke from sleep, he did as the angel of the Lord commanded him; he took her as his wife, ²⁵but had no marital relations with her until she had borne a son; and he named him Jesus.

After reading this familiar text, continue listening for new significance and insights within it.

As Matthew begins his narrative of the Messiah's birth, he further explains who Jesus is. Through the lineage of Joseph and his legal paternity, Jesus is Son of David. Through the Holy Spirit and the virginal maternity of Mary, he is Son of God. The obedient and willing responses of both Joseph and Mary are necessary for the coming of the Savior.

The couple was between the two stages of Jewish marriage. They had completed the first stage, the formal exchange of consent, made at the home of the bride's father. They were preparing for the second stage, made some months or even years later, the solemn transfer of the bride to the house of the groom. The betrothal of Mary and Joseph was a legally contracted marriage, completed before they came to live together.

Joseph became aware of Mary's pregnancy before God revealed to him its meaning and cause. Joseph knew that Mary was holy and honorable, yet he also knew that pregnancy could only be the result of either willing or forced relations with another man. According to the law given in Deuteronomy, Joseph could have exposed Mary to the humiliation of a public procedure, but he chose to quietly divorce her, without accusation, trial, punishment, and shame.

The divine revelation given in his dream cut short one agonizing choice and presented him with another, the choice to cooperate with the incredible workings of God. His choice to do "as the angel of the Lord commanded him" (v. 24) caught him up in the cosmic drama wherein heaven and earth met in the child of Mary's womb.

The conception of the child in Mary's womb was revealed to be "from the Holy Spirit" (vv. 18, 20). In the Old Testament, the Spirit of God was linked with God's creating power, the inspired words of the prophets, and God's creation anew in the last days. The work of the Holy Spirit in the womb of Mary both continued and brought to a climax God's work throughout Israel's history.

The text of the prophet Isaiah, "Look, the virgin shall conceive and bear a son, and they shall name him Emmanuel" (v. 23) was an oracle of hope given originally to the house of David in the eighth century before Christ. The dynasty of David was once again in jeopardy because of invading armies. In that bleak situation, Isaiah prophesied a divine sign of assurance, a sign guaranteeing God's continual faithfulness to David's lineage. The prophecy spoke of the approaching birth of a king, born from the dynasty of David. His birth and reign would bring restoration to the people and would be a sign that God is truly with his people.

The mother of the future king is called a young maiden in the Hebrew text, but the Greek text, the version more familiar to the early Christians, specified that the maiden was a "virgin." In the Hebrew Scriptures, Israel is often referred to as a young woman and sometimes specifically as a virgin (Amos 5:2). The later Jewish period understood Isaiah's words as a messianic prophecy, proposing that virgin Israel would give birth to the Messiah.

Matthew understood that this ancient prophecy found its fuller meaning in light of Jesus. The text fortified the faith of the early church in the messianic identity of Jesus and his virginal conception. Through the ancient text, the evangelist proclaims that Jesus is the long-awaited Savior, that he was born of Mary the virgin, and that through him God is with his people in a completely new way. Mary represents virgin Israel, implying that God's people cannot bring forth the Messiah from their own human history but only through the direct intervention of God. In these ways, Matthew's citation of Isaiah's text stresses the continuity between God's saving work throughout the ancient biblical tradition and God's new work of salvation in the Messiah's coming.

Answer this question to build your understanding:

‡ How does Mary's pregnancy indicate that Jesus is the Son of God?

Meditatio

After reflecting on the text you have read, spend some time thinking about its implications for your life. Write out your answers to these questions:

‡ What are some of the emotions felt by women when they discover they are pregnant? What mixture of feelings might Mary have felt in these moments?

‡ What is the meaning and significance in God's plan that Mary was a virgin? What does Mary's virginity tell us about Jesus?

‡ In what ways does Mary's pregnancy fulfill the hopes expressed in Isaiah's prophecy of the young maiden? What is the significance of this prophecy in my relationship with Jesus?

Oratio

Speak to God using the words of this prayer or those of your own.

God of love, you bring new hope to your people through the pregnancy of women and the birth of children. Give me a spirit of trusting confidence in your presence in the world and give me faith in Jesus, our Emmanuel.

Continue praying with confidence to the One who desires your joyful hope . . .

Contemplatio

When words fail and are no longer necessary, slowly repeat the word "Emmanuel," which means "God is with us," to lead you into contemplation. Spend some moments in quiet trust, knowing that God is with you.

After your time of silent contemplation, write a few words about your experience.

Operatio

How has this Scripture challenged me to greater trust? What can I do to demonstrate my confidence in God to those around me?

3

Elizabeth Conceives in
Her Barrenness

Lectio

As you read the Scripture and commentary, highlight or underline passages that seem most pertinent to you. These marks will help you recall your experience of hearing the Scripture and seeking to understand its significance.

LUKE 1:5–25

⁵In the days of King Herod of Judea, there was a priest named Zechariah, who belonged to the priestly order of Abijah. His wife was a descendant of Aaron, and her name was Elizabeth. ⁶Both of them were righteous before God, living blamelessly according to all the commandments and regulations of the Lord. ⁷But they had no children, because Elizabeth was barren, and both were getting on in years.

⁸Once when he was serving as priest before God and his section was on duty, ⁹he was chosen by lot, according to the custom of the priesthood, to enter the sanctuary of the Lord and offer incense. ¹⁰Now at the time of the incense offering, the whole assembly of the people was praying outside. ¹¹Then there appeared to him an angel of the Lord, standing at the right side of the altar of incense. ¹²When Zechariah saw him, he was terrified; and fear overwhelmed him.

¹³But the angel said to him, "Do not be afraid, Zechariah, for your prayer has been heard. Your wife Elizabeth will bear you a son, and you will name him John. ¹⁴You will have joy and gladness, and many will rejoice at his birth, ¹⁵for he will be great in the sight of the Lord. He must never drink wine or strong drink; even before his birth he will be filled with the Holy Spirit. ¹⁶He will turn many of the people of Israel to the Lord their God. ¹⁷With the spirit and power of Elijah he will go before him, to turn the hearts of parents to their children, and the disobedient to the wisdom of the righteous, to make ready a people prepared for the Lord." ¹⁸Zechariah said to the angel, "How will I know that this is so? For I am an old man, and my wife is getting on in years." ¹⁹The angel replied, "I am Gabriel. I stand in the presence of God, and I have been sent to speak to you and to bring you this good news. ²⁰But now, because you did not believe my words, which will be fulfilled in their time, you will become mute, unable to speak, until the day these things occur."

²¹Meanwhile the people were waiting for Zechariah, and wondered at his delay in the sanctuary. ²²When he did come out, he could not speak to them, and they realized that he had seen a vision in the sanctuary. He kept motioning to them and remained unable to speak. ²³When his time of service was ended, he went to his home.

²⁴After those days his wife Elizabeth conceived, and for five months she remained in seclusion. She said, ²⁵"This is what the Lord has done for me when he looked favorably on me and took away the disgrace I have endured among my people."

Continue your search to understand the text and its significance.

Luke's Gospel opens by spotlighting three women: Elizabeth, a barren wife; Mary, a young peasant girl; and Anna, an elderly widow. Through their faithfulness and expectation within the faith of Israel, they become Luke's model believers. By their trusting submission to God's will, they demonstrate that in God's reign the least become the greatest.

The first couple in the Gospel, Zechariah and Elizabeth, is elderly and childless, like the first couple in Israel's history, Abraham and Sarah. After years of fidelity and hope in God's promises, they are sent a divine messenger with the good news that they will have a child. Like her foremother

Sarah, who listened to the message within the tent while it was revealed to her husband, Elizabeth was at home while her husband received the divine message in the temple.

Zechariah does not believe the improbable words of the angel, and, as a result of his skepticism, he is struck silent, unable to speak until the birth of his son (v. 20). Elizabeth, in contrast, understands this new act of God and acknowledges God's unexpected grace (v. 25). Even though Zechariah is a priest, a mediator of God for the people, he is unable to recognize God's unexpected action, while Elizabeth's faith reverses our expectations and sees God's hand in the new life she bears.

Elizabeth's infertility had presented her with a situation of shame and disgrace before others. In ancient Israel's society, children were an economic necessity and the means of continuing the family line. Yet, throughout salvation history, God used such conditions as grounds for new possibilities. God's compassionate love, time and time again in the Hebrew Scriptures, is expressed through the wombs of women.

Elizabeth's five months of seclusion and Zechariah's silence offer the couple a time of contemplative reflection on the wonders of God's grace. They also create within the narrative a mood of mysterious expectation for what will happen next. The humanly impossible becomes possible with God. This pregnant elderly woman and this mute aged man represent God's possibilities within those who wait and trust. Their experience embodies the culmination of the ancient covenant and the gateway to the new.

After reading the Scripture and commentary, answer these questions to build your understanding:

✢ In what ways is Elizabeth described as a model of faithfulness and trust?

✢ What are the parallels between Elizabeth and her ancestor Sarah?

Meditatio

Look at the passages you have marked and spend some time reflecting on their significance for you.

✝ For what in my own life have I had to wait? What good can be found in waiting?

✝ Who are models of trust for me? How has their trust allowed God to work in their hearts and in the circumstances of their lives?

✝ In what way is my life barren or infertile? How might God desire to use my emptiness as the gateway to new possibilities?

Oratio

Pray to God in these words or in the words that issue from your own heart:

God of compassion, your righteous servant Elizabeth waited with faithfulness and trust in you. Teach me how to wait in joyful hope for the ways you wish to bless my life. Fill my life with a spirit of trust so that I will be confident in your loving faithfulness.

Express your trusting confidence to God in light of the possibilities ahead . . .

Contemplatio

Rest quietly in God's embrace, knowing that God can be trusted for all that you need. Feel the compassionate love that surrounds you.

After your time of silence, write a brief note about your experience of contemplation.

Operatio

The Scriptures have the power to change our attitudes from within. What new spirit does Elizabeth inspire within me that would allow me to live without shame?

4

Mary the Virgin
Conceives a Son

Lectio

Read this passage aloud so that you may simultaneously read with your eyes and listen with your ears.

LUKE 1:26–38

26In the sixth month the angel Gabriel was sent by God to a town in Galilee called Nazareth, 27to a virgin engaged to a man whose name was Joseph, of the house of David. The virgin's name was Mary. 28And he came to her and said, "Greetings, favored one! The Lord is with you." 29But she was much perplexed by his words and pondered what sort of greeting this might be. 30The angel said to her, "Do not be afraid, Mary, for you have found favor with God. 31And now, you will conceive in your womb and bear a son, and you will name him Jesus. 32He will be great, and will be called the Son of the Most High, and the Lord God will give to him the throne of his ancestor David. 33He will reign over the house of Jacob forever, and of his kingdom there will be no end." 34Mary said to the angel, "How can this be, since I am a virgin?" 35The angel said to her, "The Holy Spirit will come upon you, and the power of the Most High will overshadow you; therefore the child to be born will be holy; he will be called Son of God. ³⁶And now, your relative Elizabeth in her old age has also conceived a son; and this is the sixth month for her who was said to be barren. ³⁷For nothing will be impossible with God." ³⁸Then Mary said, "Here am I, the servant of the Lord; let it be with me according to your word." Then the angel departed from her.

After reading this inspired text, continue to listen for God's Word through this commentary.

The angel's announcement to Mary, "in the sixth month" after the announcement to Zechariah, moves us from the priestly ambience of the temple in Jerusalem to a small town in Galilee (v. 26). Nazareth was quite insignificant at the time and was never mentioned in the Scriptures of Israel. The condition of the central characters has also shifted to something radically different. Zechariah and Elizabeth were an elderly and childless couple, yet like many other righteous ones in the Hebrew Scriptures, God overcame their human inability to conceive. God's intervention in the life of Mary was unlike anything ever before in the history of salvation, as new as God's original creation. The triple insistence that Mary was a virgin highlights the fresh originality of God's action (vv. 27, 34). God's intervention was not in response to her yearning for a child, nor was it the result of anything she could have anticipated. God was doing an extraordinarily new thing in response to the watchful longing of his people.

Mary is perplexed by the angel's salutation, "Greetings, favored one! The Lord is with you" (vv. 28–29). Those previously described in Scripture as favored by God include Noah, Moses, Gideon, and Samuel. Indeed, perplexing is the reality that Mary—the woman, the young maiden, the unknown—would be graced by God to be the vehicle of salvation for God's people. Mary would have known of the great demands placed upon those who were previously favored by God. Yet, "the Lord is with you" is a pledge of God's protective and guiding presence. No matter what difficulties Mary faces, God's plans for her will be realized.

The angel declares to Mary the twofold identity of the child to be born. He will be the Messiah, the one to be given the throne of King David with an everlasting kingdom (vv. 32–33), and he will be the Son of God, because he will be conceived through the overshadowing power of God's Holy Spirit (v. 35). The church's earliest theology, reflected in Paul's writings, expresses this dual nature of Mary's child: "descended from David according to the flesh" and "Son of God with power according to the spirit" (Rom. 1:3–4). He will be a divine king. Unlike King David, whose reign was bounded by history and location, this king will reign over all people and "of his kingdom there will be no end" (v. 33). But he will come not in terrible glory, blinding light, or trumpet blast. He will come through Mary's womb, a hungry and crying child, the direct intervention of God's creating Spirit.

The sign given to Mary to confirm the angel's announcement is the pregnancy of Elizabeth, her elderly kinswoman. The secret of the past five months is now made known. The angel concludes the annunciation by expressing the trusting confidence urged upon all who receive God's promises: "For nothing will be impossible with God" (v. 37). The angel's words to Mary echo God's words to Abraham, assuring him about the future birth of his son: "Is anything too wonderful for the LORD?" At that announcement Sarah had responded with a skeptical laugh (Gen. 18:13–14). Mary, however, responds with a trusting faith and humble acceptance of God's great gift: "Here I am, the servant of the Lord; let it be with me according to your word" (v. 38). Mary received the Word of God in her heart and thus consented to conceive the Son of God in her womb. As a woman of the Word and the first to hear the gospel proclaimed, she becomes in Luke's Gospel the first and ideal disciple.

After listening to the Scripture with the ear of your heart, write out your answer to these questions:

✝ What is the reason for Luke's insistence that Mary was a virgin?

✝ How is the response of Mary different from that of Zechariah (1:12, 18)?

Meditatio

Spend some time reflecting on the meaning of the Scripture for your own life.
After meditating on each question below, write out your answers to each.

✝ How does God respond to my fears about the future? In what areas of my life do I need to hear the words of the angel: "Do not be afraid," and "Nothing will be impossible with God"?

✝ Why did God choose Mary to bring the Messiah into the world? What does this say about God's ways in my own life?

✝ How might Mary have felt about the angel's message? What might have been most difficult for her? How can her acceptance give me courage?

Oratio

Respond to God's Word to you, imitating the trusting faith and humble acceptance of Mary.

Most High God, you surprised and blessed Mary with the revelation of your plan for her life. Show me how to work with your grace in trust and humility and to respond to you like Mary, your favored daughter. Let your will be done with me according to your Word.

Continue with a prayer from your own heart . . .

Contemplatio

Ask that the power of the Holy Spirit overshadow you as you rest in God's presence. Focus on the receptive heart of Mary, who said, "Here am I . . . let it be."

After your time of silence, spend a moment writing a few notes about your experience of contemplation.

Operatio

What would I like to imitate in Mary's response to God's will: "Here am I, the servant of the Lord; let it be with me according to your word"?

5

Mary Journeys
to Visit Elizabeth

Lectio

As you read the biblical verses, listen for God's voice within the words of the inspired text.

LUKE 1:39–45

³⁹In those days Mary set out and went with haste to a Judean town in the hill country, ⁴⁰where she entered the house of Zechariah and greeted Elizabeth. ⁴¹When Elizabeth heard Mary's greeting, the child leaped in her womb. And Elizabeth was filled with the Holy Spirit ⁴²and exclaimed with a loud cry, "Blessed are you among women, and blessed is the fruit of your womb. ⁴³And why has this happened to me, that the mother of my Lord comes to me? ⁴⁴For as soon as I heard the sound of your greeting, the child in my womb leaped for joy. ⁴⁵And blessed is she who believed that there would be a fulfillment of what was spoken to her by the Lord."

Continue to search for the meaning and significance of this inspired text through these comments:

During pregnancy, mothers-to-be wait for movements within themselves and for the stirrings of new life. It is a time of expectant longing and anticipation, the emotions that the church seeks to stir within itself every Advent season. In this scene we witness the private sphere of two pregnant women supporting one another and reflecting on how God is acting within their lives. Presumably Joseph is left behind and Zechariah is still unable to speak. Mary, having received God's revelation about what God has done for Elizabeth, travels in haste to greet her kinswoman (vv. 39–40). Elizabeth, her seclusion at an end with Mary's greeting, feels the leaping of the child in her womb and receives a revelation from the Holy Spirit of what God has done for Mary.

The two women represent the meeting of the old covenant and the new covenant. Elizabeth is elderly and will have a son who will be the last great figure of ancient Israel. Mary is young and will have a son who will usher in the new age of salvation. In Mary, the new covenant reaches out to the old covenant, affirming its crucial significance in God's plan and preparing for its culmination. In Elizabeth, the old covenant recognizes its own fulfillment and honors the coming of the new. The joyful unity of these two women expresses the harmony between the traditional faith of Israel and the coming of the Savior, a completion and a new beginning of God's saving work in the world.

Elizabeth's twofold blessing praises the saving significance of Mary's obedience to God's Word among all the people of God (v. 42). First, Elizabeth proclaims of Mary, "Blessed are you among women." God has exalted Mary among all the women of the ancient covenant—Sarah, Rachel, Hannah, Deborah, Jael (Judg. 5:24), and Judith (Jth. 13:18)—for Mary has been chosen to bring forth the one awaited by all past generations. These women of Israel were instruments of God's saving will, either by bringing forth new hope through their children or by delivering God's people from their enemies. Second, Elizabeth's exclamation, "Blessed is the fruit of your womb," echoes the promise God made in the Torah to those who listened and obeyed the voice of God (Deut. 28:4). Elizabeth's double blessing honors Mary both in her own right among the other women and for the child she bears in her womb.

Elizabeth calls Mary "the mother of my Lord" (v. 43), the most exalted role of anyone in God's plan for the world's salvation. The title implies that

Jesus is the royal Messiah and that Mary is the king's mother. Among the lineage of King David, the royal mother played a central role in the birth, enthronement, and reign of each successive king. In acclaiming Mary as the Lord's "mother," she acknowledges first that Jesus was Lord from the beginning of his human existence in Mary's womb, and second that Mary remains the mother of the Lord always because she conceived and gave flesh to the one who will reign forever, human and divine, in heaven.

Elizabeth blesses Mary not only because she is blessed among women for bearing the Lord in her womb but also because she has believed the Word of God: "And blessed is she who believed that there would be a fulfillment of what was spoken to her by the Lord" (v. 45). Thus Mary is praised both as the mother of the Lord and as a model for Christian believers. Mary is the ideal disciple because she is committed to God's Word. She is a hearer and a doer of the Word. After receiving the Good News of Christ, she hastens to share that Word with another in need. She surrenders herself to God's plan; she is full of gratitude for the gifts she receives; and she has a contemplative sense of wonder at the mysteries of God.

After thinking about this encounter between Mary and Elizabeth, try to answer these questions:

✛ How do Mary and Elizabeth represent the Old and New Testaments?

✛ What does Elizabeth's declaration of Mary as "mother of my Lord" say about Mary and about her son?

Meditatio

Spend some time imaginatively placing yourself within this biblical scene as you reflect on these questions:

✝ Luke describes this scene of the meeting of two pregnant women as a joyful experience. What do I imagine to be some of the reasons for their abundant joy?

✝ What are the reasons Mary is called "blessed" in this passage? In what ways can she be a model and inspiration for me?

✝ What inspires me from the life of Elizabeth? What aspects of her joyful faith would I like to imitate?

Oratio

Respond to what you have heard in the encounter between Elizabeth and Mary as you pray to God.

God my Savior, you have raised up women of courage and faith among all the generations of your people. Elizabeth and Mary express the best in expectant trust among people in covenant with you. Help me to wait in joyful hope for the fulfillment of your saving promises.

Ask God to give you the gift of joy and hope . . .

Contemplatio

Spend some quiet moments resting in God's tender embrace, realizing that God is graciously bestowing the gifts of faith, hope, and love to you.

After some contemplative moments, write a few words about your experience.

Operatio

How did Elizabeth and Mary enrich the lives of each other? How could my life be different if I shared the intimacy of faith with a trusted relative or friend?

6

Anna the Prophet
and Herald

Lectio

Prepare to read the Scripture by asking God's Spirit to open your mind, your lips, and your heart.

LUKE 2:33–38

[33]And the child's father and mother were amazed at what was being said about him. [34]Then Simeon blessed them and said to his mother Mary, "This child is destined for the falling and the rising of many in Israel, and to be a sign that will be opposed [35]so that the inner thoughts of many will be revealed—and a sword will pierce your own soul too."

[36]There was also a prophet, Anna the daughter of Phanuel, of the tribe of Asher. She was of a great age, having lived with her husband seven years after her marriage, [37]then as a widow to the age of eighty-four. She never left the temple but worshiped there with fasting and prayer night and day. [38]At that moment she came, and began to praise God and to speak about the child to all who were looking for the redemption of Jerusalem.

After carefully listening to this Scripture with your heart, continue to explore its significance through the teaching of God's people.

Jerusalem and its temple are important for Luke's Gospel to show readers how the life of Jesus and his church are rooted in ancient Israel, its worship, and its institutions. For this reason, the Gospel begins and ends in Jerusalem, the focal point of Israel's memories and hopes. The infancy narratives continually emphasize that the family of Jesus did everything required by the law of Moses. Their observance included the precepts regarding circumcision of the child, purification of the mother after childbirth, and presentation of the firstborn. In this scene, the law, the temple, and the spirit of prophecy, all ancient expressions of the covenant, come together to form the context for God's new revelation.

Luke's description of Jesus's infancy began with an elderly, obedient man and woman, Zechariah and Elizabeth, and it ends with a similar couple, Simeon and Anna. When Mary and Joseph bring Jesus to be presented in the temple, they encounter this old man and woman, who represent Israel at its best. They are devout and righteous, at home in the temple, moved by God's Spirit, longing for the fulfillment of God's promises, and awaiting the coming of God's salvation. They demonstrate that the hope revealed in Jesus is built on memory, that God's new work is the fulfillment of old promises.

After Simeon proclaims a message of light, joy, and hope about Jesus, which brings amazement to Joseph and Mary, he then casts a dark shadow in a prophecy directed specifically to Mary (vv. 33–34). Like the other prophets of Israel, he speaks about the actions of God as well as tragic human choices. The fulfillment of God's promises will be accompanied by great costs. The response of Israel to the teaching and mission of Jesus will create great disruption and division, "the falling and the rising of many." He will be "a sign that will be opposed." The shadow of the cross already begins to fall across the joyful scenes of the Messiah's birth. He will be spurned and rejected by many, even as he is received and accepted by others.

Then, in a personal aside to Mary, Simeon states, "and a sword will pierce your own soul too," expressing the heart-rending pain she will experience for her intimate association with Jesus, both as his mother and as his first disciple (v. 35). She, who was the first to hear and receive the Good News about Jesus, must also encounter within her own soul the suffering caused by the tragic rejection of that saving news by many.

Anna, the elderly and faithful woman of Israel, is also in the temple at the presentation of Jesus (v. 36). As a "prophet" she takes her place in the Scriptures alongside other women of Israel who are described as prophets: Miriam (Exod. 15:20), Deborah (Judg. 4:4), Huldah (2 Kings 22:14), and Isaiah's wife (Isa. 8:3). Her membership "of the tribe of Asher" means that her ancestors lived in the northern area of Israel in the region of Galilee. After the exile many descendants of the northern tribes settled in Jerusalem and renewed their devotion to the temple. The specific mention of her tribe assures the reader that the characters in the narrative represent the messianic hopes of all of Israel, northern tribes as well as southern, exiles as well as inhabitants of the land.

Apparently she was a well-known figure in Jerusalem, easily remembered as the stories of Jesus's infancy were preserved in the early decades of the church. Her old age of eighty-four and her designation as a "widow" associate her with the many faithful widows we will encounter in Luke's Gospel. The text says, "She never left the temple but worshiped there with fasting and prayer night and day" (v. 37). She had been granted the desire expressed by the psalmist: "to live in the house of the LORD all the days of my life, to behold the beauty of the LORD, and to inquire in his temple" (Ps. 27:4).

As Jesus came to the temple, she praised God and began "to speak about the child to all who were looking for the redemption of Jerusalem" (v. 38). In her last days, she was able to glimpse in the young Jesus what God had in store for his people. Her longing and hoping were over, and she could now move off stage as the new era of salvation begins in the ministry of Jesus. The elderly and watchful Anna reminds us to heed the words of the psalmist: "Wait for the LORD; be strong, and let your heart take courage; wait for the LORD!" (Ps. 27:14).

Meditatio

Envision this encounter with the watchful Anna and consider the feelings that arise within you.

✝ Why does this Gospel message include both light and shadow? What does it mean to say that the cross has cast its shadow over the Christmas crib?

✝ How might Mary have felt when Simeon addressed the prophecy of the piercing sword to her? In what ways was his prophecy fulfilled through her years as the mother of Jesus?

✝ What can Anna teach me about persistent hope? What value can I find in the words of the psalmist: "Be strong, and let your heart take courage; wait for the LORD" (Ps. 27:14)?

Oratio

This narrative expresses hope, joy, sorrow, patience, and gratitude. Respond to God in prayer from the depths of your heart.

> Lord God, your servant Anna desired to worship you in the temple with prayer and fasting night and day. Place within me a longing for your presence and a yearning to pray. Help me to be patient, to live contemplatively, and to wait for you with trust.

Continue to pray to God with emotional honesty . . .

Contemplatio

Ask for the prayerful spirit of Anna, who was happy to live in God's temple night and day. Spend some moments simply being grateful for the presence of God.

After your time of contemplation, write a few words about your experience.

Operatio

Which of Anna's virtues do I admire? How could I put one of her qualities into practice in my own relationship with God?

7

Simon's Mother-in-law
Healed by Jesus

Lectio

Highlight or underline passages that seem most significant as you read the Scriptures and commentary. These marks will help you ask questions of the text and seek to understand its significance.

MARK 1:29–31

²⁹As soon as they left the synagogue, they entered the house of Simon and Andrew, with James and John. ³⁰Now Simon's mother-in-law was in bed with a fever, and they told him about her at once. ³¹He came and took her by the hand and lifted her up. Then the fever left her, and she began to serve them.

MATTHEW 8:14–15

¹⁴When Jesus entered Peter's house, he saw his mother-in-law lying in bed with a fever; ¹⁵he touched her hand, and the fever left her, and she got up and began to serve him.

LUKE 4:38–39

³⁸After leaving the synagogue he entered Simon's house. Now Simon's mother-in-law was suffering from a high fever, and they asked him about her. ³⁹Then he stood over her and rebuked the fever, and it left her. Immediately she got up and began to serve them.

After carefully reading and comparing these texts, continue to explore the meaning and significance of this narrative.

The healing of Simon's mother-in-law is one of Jesus's earliest recorded miracles, immediately following his proclamation that "the kingdom of God has come near" and the call of his first four disciples. In Mark's Gospel, probably the earliest account, the first three miracles are worked for those considered by the culture to be most lowly and needy: a man possessed by a demon, a woman, and a leper. The miracles are performed not just to amaze the crowds but as a concrete manifestation that the kingdom is breaking into the world, casting out evil and making the sick whole again.

The passage begins with a transition: "they left the synagogue" and "they entered the house" (v. 29). This does not express a rejection of the synagogue but rather the movement of Jesus's ministry from the more formal setting of Jewish life to the domestic sphere. The early church would also move from the synagogue and develop its communal life within house churches. Within the household, the church modeled its ministry on the family, calling one another brothers and sisters and centering its communal life on table fellowship. Within this domestic setting, assumed to be the domain of women in ancient culture, the function of women in roles of ministry became more significant than in the more institutional settings of Judaism.

In fact, archaeologists have excavated what they identify as the house of Simon Peter in Capernaum. Evidence suggests that it was a simple family home at the time of Jesus. Later in the first century, the walls of this house were plastered, and Christians began carving prayers in the walls, indicating it served as an early house church. The pilgrim Egeria, in the fourth century, wrote in her travel diary, "In Capernaum a house church was made out of the house of Peter, and its walls still stand today." In the fifth century, an octagonal church was built over the site.

Simon's mother-in-law, like many women of the Gospels, is not given a name. As was customary in that culture, she was identified by her closest male relative. Since she was identified with Simon (later called Peter), it is possible that she had no sons and that her husband had died. Though the text does not explicitly say she lived in the house, we can assume that she lived with the family of Simon. Mark's Gospel identifies it as the house of Simon and his brother, Andrew. The excavations reveal a cluster of rooms opening to a common courtyard that could have been occupied by the families of both brothers.

The healing is recorded in the three Synoptic Gospels with a slightly different emphasis in each. Mark says that Jesus "took her by the hand and lifted her up" (1:31) stressing the physical touch of Jesus as a Spirit-empowered healer. Because "lifted up" and "got up" is the same verb used to describe the resurrection, the Gospels show that Jesus's healing manifests the power of God's kingdom, a power that will be fully manifested in the resurrection of the dead. Both Mark and Matthew say, "the fever left her" (Mark 1:31; Matt. 8:15), suggesting that the fever was an evil power that fled at the touch of Jesus. Luke's Gospel omits the physical touch and states that Jesus "rebuked the fever" (v. 39) associating the healing with the previous healing of a man possessed by an unclean spirit. Both possession and sickness indicate the rule of evil's power, which departs under the authority of Jesus.

Each Gospel states that Peter's mother-in-law got up and "began to serve" (Mark 1:31; Matt. 8:15; Luke 4:39). On one level of meaning, we can assume that she got up to cook a meal and offer the hospitality she would have offered her guests had she not been ill. The verb, however, in all three Gospels suggests "to serve" or "to minister." It is the same verb Jesus used when he told his followers that he came "not to be served but to serve." Simon's mother-in-law is not only the first woman to be healed by Jesus but also a model for all people who are raised up by Jesus for the life of God's kingdom and respond to this new life by serving in his ministry.

The fact that Simon Peter had a mother-in-law means that he was married. Though his wife is not mentioned in this passage, Paul indicates in his writings that Peter's wife accompanied him in his missionary travels during the period of the early church (1 Cor. 9:5). Though she too remains nameless, her service must have been significant—both during the life of Jesus, when her house became the headquarters for his ministry in Galilee, and also decades later when she and her husband traveled to proclaim the gospel to distant lands.

Meditatio

Use your imagination and enter the scene yourself. Imagine the senses and feelings involved in this encounter with Jesus.

✝ What indicates to me that Jesus's healing of Simon's mother-in-law was intended to draw out more than amazement from the disciples? What is the deeper purpose of the healing?

✝ Why do the Gospels describe the response of Peter's mother-in-law after her healing? In what way have I been lifted up by Jesus to serve? What type of service suits me best as my response to the touch of Jesus?

✝ Peter's wife shared the house of Peter, which served as the home base for the ministry of Jesus. While the Gospels tell us mostly about the public life of Jesus, she experienced his domestic life after he returned each day from his ministry in Galilee. What might she have learned about Jesus during those years?

Oratio

After experiencing this account with your imagination and feelings, respond to God with the words that rise from your heart.

> Healing Lord, you touched the mother-in-law of Peter with your power and lifted her up to serve your people. Place your healing hand upon me today and lift from my life all that prevents me from serving you and your church with all my heart.

Continue to speak words that express whatever new service you desire to offer . . .

Contemplatio

Simply relax and imagine the healing hand of Jesus lifting you up. Do nothing. Say nothing. Just believe in the desire of Jesus to make you whole.

Following your contemplative prayer, write a few words describing your experience.

Operatio

Consider service as an expression of gratitude for Jesus's calling you into God's kingdom. What form of ministry best expresses your desire to serve?

8

A Little Girl
Restored to Life

Close off the distractions of the day and enter into a quiet space where you can listen to God's voice speak through the literary text.

MARK 5:21–24, 35–43

²¹When Jesus had crossed again in the boat to the other side, a great crowd gathered around him; and he was by the sea. ²²Then one of the leaders of the synagogue named Jairus came and, when he saw him, fell at his feet ²³and begged him repeatedly, "My little daughter is at the point of death. Come and lay your hands on her, so that she may be made well, and live."

²⁴So he went with him. And a large crowd followed him and pressed in on him.

³⁵While he was still speaking, some people came from the leader's house to say, "Your daughter is dead. Why trouble the teacher any further?" ³⁶But overhearing what they said, Jesus said to the leader of the synagogue, "Do not fear, only believe." ³⁷He allowed no one to follow him except Peter, James, and John, the brother of James. ³⁸When they came to the house of the leader of the synagogue, he

saw a commotion, people weeping and wailing loudly. [39]When he had entered, he said to them, "Why do you make a commotion and weep? The child is not dead but sleeping." [40]And they laughed at him. Then he put them all outside, and took the child's father and mother and those who were with him, and went in where the child was. [41]He took her by the hand and said to her, "Talitha cum," which means, "Little girl, get up!" [42]And immediately the girl got up and began to walk about (she was twelve years of age). At this they were overcome with amazement. [43]He strictly ordered them that no one should know this, and told them to give her something to eat.

Continue exploring the full meaning and significance of this narrative through these remarks.

After Jesus crosses the Sea of Galilee back to the Jewish territory, a leading official of the synagogue named Jairus approaches Jesus with worry and fear. His daughter is seriously ill and near death. It is unusual for a representative of the religious leadership to approach Jesus, but as a desperate parent he seeks the help of Jesus, whose healing power has become well known. He relinquishes his status as a synagogue leader and casts aside his public dignity, falling at the feet of Jesus and begging for his help. He pleads for Jesus to come to his house and lay his hands on his daughter, a gesture of healing that Jesus often used and that the early church continued.

Jesus goes with the man but is pressed in by a large crowd. The Gospel writer inserts here the account of the woman with the hemorrhage (vv. 25–34), requiring a long delay while Jesus responds to her desperate needs. Meanwhile, Jairus waits with growing fear that his daughter's life is fading at his home. Before Jesus finishes with the woman, the dreaded news is brought to Jairus: "Your daughter is dead. Why trouble the teacher any further?" (v. 35). The messenger is suggesting that Jesus is only a teacher, and death marks the limit of whatever power he may have. But Jesus, overhearing the message, urges Jairus not to lose heart: "Do not fear, only believe" (v. 36).

Coming to the house, they see that the crowd is already engaged in the rituals of mourning, loudly weeping and wailing. It appears that death has taken possession of the scene. Jesus's statement that "the child is not dead but sleeping" seems like nonsense, and the crowd laughs at him (vv. 39–40). So Jesus expels the crowd from the house, leaving only the girl's mother and father and Jesus's three closest disciples. He is creating a house of faith, a domestic environment in which belief in the saving power of Jesus can overcome even death in order to bring life to the girl. The writer preserves the original Aramaic words of Jesus as he takes the girl by the hand and speaks to her directly, telling her to arise (v. 41). The girl then immediately gets up and begins walking around, while the witnesses look on in amazement.

We don't know many details about this young girl. Because her father was a leading official of the synagogue, she was evidently from a privileged home with status in Jewish society. The girl had an influential male advocate in her father, who pleaded her cause. Yet, we see that despite Jesus's mission on behalf of this man at the top of the honor scale, he delays his journey to tend to the needs of a destitute woman. We are also told by the narrator that the girl is twelve years of age (v. 42). This was the usual age of puberty and near the time when a girl was given by her father in marriage. With high infant mortality and low life expectancy, women were expected to marry as soon as they could begin bearing children. But this girl would not have been able to marry, have children, or have a future had Jesus not drawn her back into the realm of life and possibility.

Jesus's strange order at the end of the account, that no one should know about this event, seemingly demanded the impossible. The girl's mother and father could not refrain from telling the crowd what had happened to their daughter. Yet, the command to tell no one, found often in Mark's Gospel after accounts of Jesus's miracles, suggests that Jesus does not want to be known as a wonder worker. Though Jesus does indeed heal by the power of God, faith in him must not be dependent on miracles. Mark's Gospel demonstrates that the true nature of Jesus's identity and mission can only be understood at the cross. Disciples cannot understand who he truly is until they witness his crucifixion and death. Faith based on wonders is too conditional and fragile to sustain Christian disciples. Belief in Jesus must be rooted in a faith much deeper than the simple belief that God will work in our lives in the ways we expect and demand.

Meditatio

Spend some time allowing the text to interact with your own world of memories, fears, hopes, and expectations, and then ask yourself what the passage means to you.

‡ What might have been the emotions in the heart of Jairus as he begged Jesus for his healing touch? How must he have felt when the messenger announced that his daughter was dead?

‡ What is Jesus's reaction to the news that the girl is dead? In what situations do I need to hear the words of Jesus, "Do not fear, only believe" (v. 36)?

‡ In what ways does this account lead me to a deeper faith? Why does Jesus not want to be identified primarily as a wonder worker?

8 - A Little Girl Restored to Life • 49

Oratio

Choose the words or phrases that have most spoken to your heart in this passage. Use these words as the foundation of your own heartfelt prayer to God.

> Compassionate Lord, you desire the healing and wholeness of your people. Help me to nurture a deeper faith within myself so that I can respond to the ways you want to work in my life.

Continue to pray from your heart using the words and ideas of the Scriptures . . .

Contemplatio

Slowly repeat the words of Jesus, "Do not fear, only believe," allowing these words to gradually move you into a confident trust in the possibilities for your life.

Following this experience of contemplative prayer, write a few words describing your trusting prayer.

Operatio

Jesus takes each of us by the hand and says, "Arise." How does my experience of this passage enable me to live this day in a new way?

9

The Woman Healed
of a Hemorrhage

Lectio

Read this text as if for the first time. Notice the sights, movement, and emotions of the passage. Place yourself within it and draw upon its healing power.

MARK 5:25–34

[25]Now there was a woman who had been suffering from hemorrhages for twelve years. [26]She had endured much under many physicians, and had spent all that she had; and she was no better, but rather grew worse. [27]She had heard about Jesus, and came up behind him in the crowd and touched his cloak, [28]for she said, "If I but touch his clothes, I will be made well." [29]Immediately her hemorrhage stopped; and she felt in her body that she was healed of her disease. [30]Immediately aware that power had gone forth from him, Jesus turned about in the crowd and said, "Who touched my clothes?" [31]And his disciples said to him, "You see the crowd pressing in on you; how can you say, 'Who touched me?'" [32]He looked all around to see who had done it. [33]But the woman, knowing what had happened to her, came in fear and trembling, fell down before him, and told him the whole truth. [34]He said to her, "Daughter, your faith has made you well; go in peace, and be healed of your disease."

Continue to seek the full meaning of the healing narrative you have just experienced.

While Jesus is on his way to the home of Jairus and being pressed in by the large crowd, a woman emerges from the throng in an attempt to reach Jesus. The woman's malady is described literally as a continuous flow of blood, which she has suffered for twelve years (v. 25). Commentators suggest that her problem is a menstrual disorder or a chronic uterine hemorrhage. Her illness is serious and long-standing. Apparently she had some wealth, at one time, because she could afford the care of physicians. But their ineffective treatment over many years has drained her of her finances, and her condition has only grown worse. She is now destitute, debilitated, and desperate.

The woman has heard reports about the healing power of Jesus, and this has given her hope and courage. Unable to approach Jesus and request a healing, the woman works her way through the jostling swarm and approaches Jesus from behind. She believes that if she only touches his clothes she will be healed. When she reaches out and touches his cloak, "Immediately her hemorrhage stopped; and she felt in her body that she was healed of her disease" (v. 29). The healing takes place solely at the woman's initiative and follows immediately upon her touching Jesus's garment, the only healing in the Gospels that occurs without the expressed intent of Jesus.

Jesus is instantly aware that healing power has gone forth from him (v. 30). His attire is certainly not possessed of magical properties. It is the power of the Spirit at work through Jesus that has brought her healing, but it is the faith of the woman that accesses that power. Jesus insists on knowing who has summoned his healing power, wanting to make personal contact with the woman and draw her into a relationship with himself. The woman, knowing that she has encountered divine power, falls down before Jesus in fear and trembling. Yet, Jesus helps her to find her voice and to tell her story, "the whole truth" about her life (v. 33). In response, Jesus praises her bold and assertive action, affirming the critical role of her own faith in securing her healing.

Jesus's parting words to the woman can also be translated, "Your faith has saved you." Her healed body and her renewed spirit attest to what

Jesus has done for her. The miracle involves far more than physical healing. Jesus calls her "daughter" (v. 34), claiming her as family, and brings her into a saving relationship with himself. He tells her to "go in peace," in *shalom*—in Hebrew, the wholeness, complete well-being, and salvation that only God can bring.

The Gospel writer inserts this passage of the woman healed of the hemorrhage within the passage about the daughter of Jairus. By intertwining these scenes, Mark creates a rich narrative text and allows each scene to shed light on the other. Both passages are full of visual details and human touches that allow us to compare and contrast the stories of two women who encountered Jesus. The little girl has enjoyed twelve years of advantage as the daughter of an honored synagogue ruler, while the woman has suffered twelve years of destitution. Both are given new life by Jesus and offered new possibilities for their future. The two parents are overjoyed that their daughter is brought back to life, while the woman, who seems to have no family, is now called "daughter" by Jesus. The woman with the flow of blood has probably been unable to have children because of her disease; the little girl faces death at the age when she is able to have children. Both women are restored by Jesus to their life-giving capacity.

After reading the Scripture and commentary, answer these questions to help focus your thoughts:

✝ What is the difference between the powers of Jesus and magical powers?

✝ Why did Jesus insist on finding the person who touched his clothes?

Meditatio

Try to personalize God's message by allowing this passage to resonate with your own hopes and dreams.

‡ What does this account teach me about the empowering presence of Jesus? How can I allow him to make me more assertive and bold in my faith?

‡ The woman takes responsibility for her life and initiative for her own healing. What can I learn from her for my own life?

‡ The story of this woman is narrated in such a way as to empower those who hear it. In what way does my hearing this account empower my life?

Oratio

Speak these words of prayer in response to the voice of Jesus you have heard in the Gospel.

Teacher and Lord, you look with compassion upon all who are suffering and in need of healing. Give me a compassionate heart for those who are poor or sick in body or in spirit. Make me an instrument of your healing and peace in the lives of others.

Continue praying to God using the words that come to you after meditating on this passage...

Contemplatio

Spend a few moments of silence, asking God to mold your heart and to make you compassionate like his Son.

Spend a few moments writing about your contemplative prayer.

Operatio

What courage does this story bring out in me? How does the account of the healed woman empower me to take responsibility for my life? In what way can I be more assertive today?

10

Herodias Schemes
with Her Daughter

*Read this familiar passage as if for the first time, without any preconceived
ideas, expecting new insights and surprises.*

MARK 6:14–29

[14]King Herod heard of it, for Jesus' name had become known.
Some were saying, "John the baptizer has been raised from the dead;
and for this reason these powers are at work in him." [15]But others
said, "It is Elijah." And others said, "It is a prophet, like one of the
prophets of old." [16]But when Herod heard of it, he said, "John, whom
I beheaded, has been raised."

[17]For Herod himself had sent men who arrested John, bound him,
and put him in prison on account of Herodias, his brother Philip's wife,
because Herod had married her. [18]For John had been telling Herod, "It
is not lawful for you to have your brother's wife." [19]And Herodias had
a grudge against him, and wanted to kill him. But she could not, [20]for
Herod feared John, knowing that he was a righteous and holy man,
and he protected him. When he heard him, he was greatly perplexed;
and yet he liked to listen to him. [21]But an opportunity came when
Herod on his birthday gave a banquet for his courtiers and officers
and for the leaders of Galilee. [22]When his daughter Herodias came in
and danced, she pleased Herod and his guests; and the king said to

the girl, "Ask me for whatever you wish, and I will give it." ²³And he solemnly swore to her, "Whatever you ask me, I will give you, even half of my kingdom." ²⁴She went out and said to her mother, "What should I ask for?" She replied, "The head of John the baptizer." ²⁵Immediately she rushed back to the king and requested, "I want you to give me at once the head of John the Baptist on a platter." ²⁶The king was deeply grieved; yet out of regard for his oaths and for the guests, he did not want to refuse her. ²⁷Immediately the king sent a soldier of the guard with orders to bring John's head. He went and beheaded him in the prison, ²⁸brought his head on a platter, and gave it to the girl. Then the girl gave it to her mother. ²⁹When his disciples heard about it, they came and took his body, and laid it in a tomb.

After entering this scene with your mind and heart, continue exploring its implications and significance.

Herod's curiosity about Jesus leads to a flashback narrative of the death of John the Baptist. This account is often depicted in painting, opera, and film. The chilling tale of court intrigue includes the vengeful Herodias, the charming young dancer, the spineless Herod, the privileged leaders of Galilean society, the uncompromising John the Baptist, and the ruthless executioner. Herod's guilt-ridden paranoia leads him to imagine that Jesus is John the Baptist returned from the dead to haunt him (v. 16). The nightmarish scenario that follows recounts the gruesome story of John's beheading.

The Herod described in this account is Herod Antipas, the son of Herod the Great. He was the ruler of Galilee during the life of Jesus. Herodias, his wife, had originally been married to Herod's half-brother. In that marriage, she had a daughter, Salome, the young woman portrayed in this account. Herodias divorced her first husband in order to marry Herod. According to the record of tangled relationships among the descendents of Herod the Great, Herodias was not only Herod's sister-in-law but also his niece.

This second marriage would have been judged incestuous and forbidden according to the law of Moses: "You shall not uncover the nakedness of your [living] brother's wife" (Lev. 18:16), and "If a man takes his brother's wife, it is impurity" (Lev. 20:21). The Gospels make clear that John was imprisoned because he reproved this incestuous and unlawful marriage (vv. 17–18). Herodias long desired to kill John because of the bitter resentment she felt for him (v. 19). Yet, she was unable to fulfill her wish because of Herod's ambiguous relationship with John. He feared John's influence among the people, yet he was also captivated by him (v. 20). Though opposite from John in every way, Herod liked to listen to him, and he knew that John was a righteous and holy man. Herodias bided her time, waiting for her opportunity to do away with John.

On Herod's birthday, he throws a banquet for the leading men of Galilee in one of his three luxurious palaces. The list of guests highlights the contrast between worldly power and John, the prophet in the wilderness (v. 21). The girl who dances into the banquet hall is described in most translations as "the daughter of Herodias," the woman we know from other historical sources as Salome (v. 22). Perhaps urged on by her conniving mother, Salome dances seductively before the inebriated gathering of men. The blustering Herod, wanting to dazzle his guests with his magnanimity, then promises her anything she wishes. When Salome confers with her mother, Herodias seizes upon her husband's foolish promise. Salome rushes back into Herod's presence and makes her shocking and grisly request: "the head of John the Baptist on a platter" (v. 25). The head is to be served up at once as one more dish at the banquet, leaving no time for Herod to sober up or deal with his wife in the morning. Though he is "deeply grieved," Herod reluctantly carries out the woman's wish because he does not want to renege on his promise in front of his prominent guests (v. 26). So upon orders from Herod, the soldiers behead John in prison and bring the head on a platter to Salome, who then gives it to Herodias. The disciples of John then come and bring his body to a tomb.

In the way that Mark fashions the narrative, the fate of John the forerunner anticipates that of Jesus. Both beheading and crucifixion are types of executions designed to defame and humiliate their victims. John's death sentence by Herod is carried out like Jesus's condemnation to death by Pontius Pilate. Both rulers are favorably impressed by the prophetic figures whose lives they would prefer to spare. Both are manipulated and become reluctant protagonists in a drama beyond their control. The faithful disciples who place the bodies of both John and Jesus in their tombs can also expect to become victims of power structures distorted by fear, envy, ambition, and compromise.

Meditatio

Think about what God is teaching you in this passage. Consider what you are learning about God's ways.

‡ In addition to the stories of faithful women, why do the Gospel writers include accounts of women who show shocking and reprehensible qualities?

‡ What was the predicament of Herod after he made his rash oath to Salome? What other response could he have given? How might he have felt about his actions the next day?

‡ How have I responded to someone in my past who confronted me about something wrong in my life? Has my response been more like that of Herodias, bitter and vengeful, or like that of Herod, curious and willing to listen?

Oratio

Pray for the gift of mercy and compassion, that your own heart might reflect the heart of God.

> God of justice and mercy, your prophets of old, like John the Baptist, denounced oppression and announced the righteousness of your kingdom. Teach me to listen to your prophets and those who challenge my lifestyle and my complacency. Help me to be always reforming my life.

Continue praying for the grace of change and renewal . . .

Contemplatio

In quiet and stillness, allow God to work within you, opening your mind and heart to be changed by his holy presence.

Write a few words about this experience of contemplative prayer.

Operatio

Lectio divina is a way of letting God's Word shape us and change us. How have I been molded and transformed by the Word of God in this Scripture?

11

The Canaanite Woman and Her Daughter

Lectio

Listen to the words of Scripture with the ear of your heart.

MATTHEW 15:21–28

21Jesus left that place and went away to the district of Tyre and Sidon. 22Just then a Canaanite woman from that region came out and started shouting, "Have mercy on me, Lord, Son of David; my daughter is tormented by a demon." 23But he did not answer her at all. And his disciples came and urged him, saying, "Send her away, for she keeps shouting after us." 24He answered, "I was sent only to the lost sheep of the house of Israel." 25But she came and knelt before him, saying, "Lord, help me." 26He answered, "It is not fair to take the children's food and throw it to the dogs." 27She said, "Yes, Lord, yet even the dogs eat the crumbs that fall from their masters' table." 28Then Jesus answered her, "Woman, great is your faith! Let it be done for you as you wish." And her daughter was healed instantly.

Continue listening to this inspired narrative while seeking its fuller meaning through this commentary.

The encounter between the Canaanite woman and Jesus is about crossing boundaries. Jesus has traversed the border separating the Jewish area of Galilee and entered the Gentile territory of Tyre and Sidon. The two characters have broken the barrier between bitter enemies, the Jews and their ancient rivals, the Canaanites. The woman breaks through the barrier that prevented women from approaching unknown males. Her concern for her daughter leads her to break all the established rules of conduct for well-mannered women. By intruding into the company of men and insisting on a hearing, she crosses the boundary from stereotypical male dominance and female submissiveness to a new model for male-female relationships.

Matthew depicts the encounter in the form of a dialogue. The Canaanite woman speaks with her own voice, addressing Jesus three times. She is clearly the protagonist, initiating each movement of the account, while Jesus plays the role of the respondent. When the woman shouts out and pleads for mercy upon herself and her demon-tormented daughter, Jesus responds with a silent rebuff. Apparently the woman continued to follow Jesus and his disciples, crying out behind them (v. 23). Annoyed by her behavior, the disciples urge Jesus to deal with her so that she will go away. Jesus then responds by stating his understanding of the divine mission he has embraced: "I was sent only to the lost sheep of the house of Israel" (v. 24). Jesus has an urgent sense of his mission to the people of Israel, and since the woman does not belong to the Jewish people, Jesus states that his mission is not for Gentiles.

Refusing to accept being ignored, the woman comes to the front side of the group and kneels before Jesus, effectively creating a roadblock in the way (v. 25). The woman is at the end of her rope, and, in one of the most moving gestures of the Gospel, simply begs, "Lord, help me." She is absolutely confident that Jesus can heal her daughter if he is so inclined. But the response of Jesus seems shockingly heartless: "It is not fair to take the children's food and throw it to the dogs" (v. 26). His words, probably reflecting a common saying, compare Jews to the children of a family and Gentiles to scavenging dogs. Jesus cannot divert food to the Gentiles that is meant for the children of Israel, whom he has a mission to feed. While some commentators suggest that Jesus said these words with a twinkle in his eye or a tongue in his cheek, it is hard to imagine that these words would be anything less than insulting to their Gentile hearer.

With relentless persistence, the woman then cleverly adapts the metaphor of Jesus's saying to her own situation: "Yes, Lord, yet even the dogs eat the crumbs that fall from their masters' table" (v. 27). In Greek culture, dogs were often the household pets and were present under the table during the family meals. The children would often share their food with the dogs. Surely the children of Israel, she thought, could share some of God's abundance with the Gentile dogs. Touché. The woman's quick and charming wit marks the only time in the Gospel when Jesus is outdone in verbal repartee. Her courageous and persistent faith brings about a complete change. Jesus praises her response, and her daughter is instantly healed.

The Canaanite woman acknowledges the priority and urgency of Jesus's mission to Israel but persistently asks for attention to the Gentiles also. She shifts Jesus's image of frugality, in which there is only enough food for the children, to an image of abundance, in which the food on the table is so plentiful that there is enough to feed the dogs beneath. By addressing him continuously as "Lord," she insists that he is Lord not only of Jews but of Gentiles as well. Jesus honors the woman for her unshakable faith in him, her insight into this inclusive power, and her understanding of the wideness of God's mercy.

This woman's faith foreshadows the response of the Gentiles to the gospel in the early church, a faith that crosses boundaries and overcomes traditional barriers that Jesus himself explicitly removes after his resurrection, commissioning his followers to "go therefore and make disciples of all nations" (28:19). Jesus's granting of her request approves the woman's attitude and provides for the early church a warrant for its mission to the Gentiles by grounding that mission in the earthly ministry of Jesus himself. The Canaanite woman provides for future generations the model of the outsider, the woman who challenges anyone who would set boundaries and limits to those who would be called sons and daughters of God.

Use your imagination and enter the scene yourself. Reflect on these questions from the viewpoint of your own life.

✝ The story of the Canaanite woman was included in the Gospel so that future generations would see themselves in her. What encouragement do I find in the account of this woman?

✝ The fact that Jesus extended himself to a Gentile instructs the Christian community to do so also. What boundaries do I need to cross and what barriers do I need to dismantle as a disciple of Jesus?

✝ Many commentators insist that Jesus learned from his encounter with the woman and changed his mind as a result. In what way does this understanding of Jesus challenge me? What in this account most indicates the humanity of Jesus?

Oratio

Respond in prayer to the inspired Word you have heard in the Gospel, knowing that God knows you intimately and cares about your every need.

> Lord, Son of David, have mercy on me. My prayers echo the cries of the woman in the Gospel pleading for her beloved daughter. Help me to imitate her refusal to give up, and give me a courageous and persistent faith in your presence.

Continue to pray like the Canaanite woman for yourself and others . . .

Contemplatio

In your imagination, kneel before Jesus and simply repeat the words of the Canaanite woman, "Lord, help me." In quiet contemplation, feel the encouraging and uplifting presence of Jesus ministering to you.

Write a few words about your experience of contemplative prayer.

Operatio

How does the Canaanite woman inspire me to change? What barriers can she encourage me to cross? What boundaries does she persuade me to dismantle?

12

The Mother of
James and John

*Slowly speak the words of the sacred text aloud. Read the text with your eyes
and hear it with your ears.*

MATTHEW 20:20–28

[20]Then the mother of the sons of Zebedee came to him with her
sons, and kneeling before him, she asked a favor of him. [21]And he said
to her, "What do you want?" She said to him, "Declare that these two
sons of mine will sit, one at your right hand and one at your left, in
your kingdom." [22]But Jesus answered, "You do not know what you
are asking. Are you able to drink the cup that I am about to drink?"
They said to him, "We are able." [23]He said to them, "You will indeed
drink my cup, but to sit at my right hand and at my left, this is not
mine to grant, but it is for those for whom it has been prepared by
my Father."

[24]When the ten heard it, they were angry with the two brothers.
[25]But Jesus called them to him and said, "You know that the rulers of
the Gentiles lord it over them, and their great ones are tyrants over
them. [26]It will not be so among you; but whoever wishes to be great

among you must be your servant, [27]and whoever wishes to be first among you must be your slave; [28]just as the Son of Man came not to be served but to serve, and to give his life a ransom for many."

Continue listening to the text for its full implications as you consider these comments.

We don't know what Zebedee did after his sons, James and John, left him behind in the fishing boat and followed Jesus. We can presume he hired more help and continued his fishing business in Capernaum. But we do know that Zebedee's wife eventually became a disciple of Jesus. Matthew's Gospel mentions her as the traveling band of disciples leaves Galilee and nears Jerusalem. Jesus has just taken his twelve disciples aside and told them of his coming passion and crucifixion. Then "the mother of the sons of Zebedee" comes to Jesus with her sons, James and John. Kneeling before Jesus, she makes a request of him that indicates a failure to understand the nature of his mission, a mistake that seems to be made by both his male and his female disciples.

The mother's request seems to be prompted by Jesus's own promise that his twelve disciples will sit on twelve thrones, presiding over the twelve tribes of Israel in the age to come (19:28). The mother of James and John requests that her two sons sit one at the left and the other at the right of Jesus in his kingdom (v. 21). She expects that Jesus will rule over his messianic kingdom, and she wants her sons to have the positions of greatest prominence and power, to the right and left of his throne. The request shows how little these companions of Jesus have advanced in their understanding of Jesus and his reign. The response of Jesus indicates how contrary is the desire for status and prestige to the way of Jesus.

Jesus asks if they can drink the cup he will drink, that is, share in the destiny of suffering he will experience in Jerusalem. Their self-confident, "we are able" (v. 22), is much too assured, for the Gospel will soon demonstrate their failure in the starkest verse of the passion narrative: "Then all the disciples deserted him and fled" (26:56).

The anger of the other ten disciples at James and John should not be interpreted as virtuous indignation at the brothers' ambition (v. 24). Rather, the ten are expressing jealous chagrin at being outmaneuvered by the two. But Jesus gathers them all together to explain the role of authority in the community of his kingdom. The contrast could not be sharper between the way that secular rulers exercise power and what should prevail among his disciples. The Christian ideal is servant-leadership. If the mother of Zebedee's sons had wanted her boys to be great, she should have asked that they be assigned the role of servant and slave in the kingdom. The final words of Jesus connect the service of a disciple with his own mission (v. 28). He came "not to be served but to serve," to give his life for women and men, drawing them into God's reign.

Matthew's Gospel shows that Jesus's lesson on the necessity of suffering was not lost on the mother of James and John. Matthew's crucifixion account notes that "the mother of the sons of Zebedee" was among the women looking on from a distance as Jesus died on the cross (27:56). Unlike the male disciples who fled before the crucifixion, the mother of James and John seemed to have grasped Jesus's lesson on discipleship. Faithful and self-giving, she will wait with Jesus at his crucifixion, remaining with him at his death and beyond.

Now that you have listened to God's Word in the Scriptures, answer these questions about the text:

‡ What did the mother of James and John not understand about the nature of Jesus's kingdom?

‡ How does Zebedee's wife demonstrate that she is a better learner than her sons?

Meditatio

Think about the ways this passage speaks to your desire to follow Jesus. Reflect on these questions in order to understand the text's personal message for you.

‡ Why do we so often hear about the discipleship of James and John but so seldom hear about that of their mother? Why is she a disciple we might want to honor and imitate?

‡ What request of Jesus might this mother have made for her sons after the resurrection? How might the experience of Jesus's passion have changed her understanding of her sons' mission?

‡ What lessons does the mother of James and John have to teach me today about motherhood and discipleship?

Oratio

Having learned from the mother of James and John what request not to make from Jesus, ask him now to make you his disciple.

> Lord Jesus, you came to serve and to give your life for others. Keep me free from the desire for status, honor, and power. Teach me how to be your disciple in the world, to care for the needs of others, and to serve your kingdom.

Continue to make whatever requests arise from within you . . .

Contemplatio

Spend a few moments in silence, asking God to mold you from within into a worthy disciple of his Son.

Write a few words about this contemplative experience.

Operatio

How difficult is it for me to follow Jesus's teachings to be a servant and slave in his kingdom? What has to change in my life for me to be a servant-leader?

13

The Widow of Nain
Mourns Her Only Son

Lectio

Breathe in, being filled with the presence of God's Spirit. Breathe out, letting go of all that could distract you from this sacred time. Begin reading when you feel ready to hear God's voice.

LUKE 7:11–17

[11]Soon afterwards he went to a town called Nain, and his disciples and a large crowd went with him. [12]As he approached the gate of the town, a man who had died was being carried out. He was his mother's only son, and she was a widow; and with her was a large crowd from the town. [13]When the Lord saw her, he had compassion for her and said to her, "Do not weep." [14]Then he came forward and touched the bier, and the bearers stood still. And he said, "Young man, I say to you, rise!" [15]The dead man sat up and began to speak, and Jesus gave him to his mother. [16]Fear seized all of them; and they glorified God, saying, "A great prophet has risen among us!" and "God has looked favorably on his people!" [17]This word about him spread throughout Judea and all the surrounding country.

After listening carefully to the narrative with your mind and heart, continue exploring its meaning through these words.

Luke's Gospel contains a number of stories of women that are not found in the other Gospels. Often a passage about a man is paired with an account depicting a woman, as if to insist that both are equally included in the blessings of God's kingdom. This narrative of the widow who lost her son to death is unique to Luke's Gospel, but it is paired with the story of Jairus, who lost his daughter to death. Luke notes in this narrative that the widow's dead son was her "only son" (v. 12), and in the account of Jairus, which Luke inherited from Mark's account, Luke adds that the girl was his "only daughter" (Luke 8:42).

The widow never speaks in this account; she remains a voiceless object of sympathy. She makes no plea of Jesus; she is simply there with the lifeless body of her son. Yet, her quiet sorrow speaks eloquently. Her silent tears move Jesus to compassion. She is like so many modern women who have lost sons to the horror of war, the techniques of torture, retribution shootings, and incurable disease. Their quiet grief has the power to stir empathy and move others to seek justice and mercy.

Throughout the biblical tradition, widows and orphans were the particular objects of pity and compassion. A woman was passed on from the care of her father, to her husband, to her son. A woman without father, husband, or son was destitute, lacking any means of support. A childless widow, like a parentless child, represented an extreme form of defenselessness. Thus, Luke describes true desperation when he states that this widow from Nain was mourning her only son. In addition to her emotional loss, she would no longer have a source of sustenance or a means of protection.

Overwhelmed with grief and anxiety about the future, this woman seems to be beyond hope. Her son is dead and about to be buried. The large crowd with her presents a strong contrast to the obvious loneliness of the widow, isolated in her sadness and desolation. There is no mention in this account of faith; Jesus does not ask it and the woman does not offer it. She seems empty of any ability to express her needs or her prayer.

The initiative to raise the widow's son comes completely from Jesus. There is no request, no plea for mercy. No one intercedes for the woman.

Luke simply says, "When the Lord saw her, he had compassion for her" (v. 13). Jesus speaks to her and says simply, "Do not weep." The focus is on Jesus and the power of God at work in him. Jesus touches the bier on which the body of the young man is being carried, commands him to rise, and gives him to his mother. Both the son and the mother are restored to life and hope.

Luke forms his Gospel account so as to evoke the memory of the Old Testament account of the prophet Elijah as he raises to life the son of the widow at Zarephath (1 Kings 17:8–24). In both narratives, a widow grieves the death of her only son. Both sons are raised to life and given to their mothers by one who acts and speaks for God. The response of the crowd to Jesus, "A great prophet has risen among us!" (v. 16) indicates that Jesus is in a direct line with the prophets of old, but he is more than a prophet. He is the one who inaugurates the new age of salvation. Through the testimony of the crowd, word about Jesus spreads throughout Judea and the entire region.

Now that you have heard the story of the grieving widow, answer these questions about the text:

‡ Why did the death of her son provoke both grief and anxiety in the widow?

‡ In what way does the Gospel writer demonstrate Jesus's motives for raising the son of this poor widow?

‡ How is Jesus shown to be a great prophet in line with the prophets of old?

Meditatio

Reflect on how the inspired text speaks God's Word to the circumstances of your own life.

‡ Put yourself in the place of the widow. What is behind and beneath her silent grieving?

‡ What are some of the struggles and heartaches borne by women today because of the inadequacies of our society?

‡ Why does the Bible describe widows and orphans as especially important to God? What does this say about the characteristics of our God?

Oratio

Speak to God in response to the words, ideas, and images from the reading. Use these or similar words.

Compassionate God, you look upon the silent grief and the anxious fears of your people everywhere. Help me to realize that you are the God who heeds the cry of widows and orphans. Give me a spirit of compassion for your suffering people modeled on the heart of your Son.

Continue praying as you respond to God, who has first spoken to you . . .

Contemplatio

In wordless silence, receptively allow God to fill your heart with his healing and compassionate presence.

Write a few words about your experience of God in silence.

Operatio

Whom does the widow represent today? In what way does her plight move me to action?

14

The Woman Who Showed Great Love

Lectio

In a quiet place, read the Scripture slowly and carefully, asking God's Spirit to guide you in your understanding.

LUKE 7:36–50

[36]One of the Pharisees asked Jesus to eat with him, and he went into the Pharisee's house and took his place at the table. [37]And a woman in the city, who was a sinner, having learned that he was eating in the Pharisee's house, brought an alabaster jar of ointment. [38]She stood behind him at his feet, weeping, and began to bathe his feet with her tears and to dry them with her hair. Then she continued kissing his feet and anointing them with the ointment. [39]Now when the Pharisee who had invited him saw it, he said to himself, "If this man were a prophet, he would have known who and what kind of woman this is who is touching him—that she is a sinner." [40]Jesus spoke up and said to him, "Simon, I have something to say to you." "Teacher," he replied, "Speak." [41]"A certain creditor had two debtors; one owed five hundred denarii, and the other fifty. [42]When they could not pay, he canceled the debts for both of them. Now which of them will love him more?" [43]Simon answered, "I suppose the one for whom he canceled the greater

debt." And Jesus said to him, "You have judged rightly." [44]Then turning toward the woman, he said to Simon, "Do you see this woman? I entered your house; you gave me no water for my feet, but she has bathed my feet with her tears and dried them with her hair. [45]You gave me no kiss, but from the time I came in she has not stopped kissing my feet. [46]You did not anoint my head with oil, but she has anointed my feet with ointment. [47]Therefore, I tell you, her sins, which were many, have been forgiven; hence she has shown great love. But the one to whom little is forgiven, loves little." [48]Then he said to her, "Your sins are forgiven." [49]But those who were at the table with him began to say among themselves, "Who is this who even forgives sins?" [50]And he said to the woman, "Your faith has saved you; go in peace."

Continue exploring the meaning and significance of this passage through this commentary.

Many who witnessed the work of Jesus took offense at his words and deeds. He was called "a friend of tax collectors and sinners" (7:34), one who "welcomes sinners and eats with them" (15:2), provoking scandal among those who had different expectations about the appropriate demeanor of the Messiah. Desiring those who saw his saving work to understand him and accept his divine mission, Jesus said, "Blessed is anyone who takes no offense at me" (7:23). Yet, he met increasing opposition, especially among the religious elite, because of the healing and forgiveness he offered. In this account, which takes place in the house of a Pharisee, the man takes offense at the behavior of Jesus, who accepts this woman's extravagant display of gratitude and love.

Jesus and Simon the Pharisee are eating in the customary style, reclining on their side with their feet pointing away from the table. This explains the position of the woman, standing behind Jesus at his feet (v. 38). Her lavish gestures—bathing his feet with her tears, drying them with her hair, kissing his feet and rubbing them with ointment—are interpreted quite differently by Simon and by Jesus, two contrasting religious authorities. The Pharisee, knowing the woman is a sinner, assumes that Jesus will shrink back from her and expel her from the room. He concludes that Jesus must not be a prophet after all, since he does not know the character of this woman (v. 39). The irony is that not only does Jesus know the heart of this woman, but he also knows the thoughts of his host.

In order to help Simon understand his way of seeing this woman, Jesus tells a parable (vv. 41–42). Both sums of money owed by the two debtors are substantial, since a denarius was the wage for a full day of labor. But the one whose debt was ten times the amount of the other was, of course, more grateful to the one who forgave the debt. The woman's actions are an expression of gratitude that her many sins have been forgiven. Jesus shows that the real contrast in the scene is between Simon and the woman in their response to Jesus. Even though Jesus is a guest in Simon's house, the host has shown his thoughtlessness by failing to provide any of the customary demonstrations of hospitality. It is the woman who extends real hospitality through her expression of gratefulness, "hence she has shown great love" (v. 47).

Though the text does not say what sort of sins the woman had committed in the past, many commentators presume that she was a prostitute. Yet, neither her clothing, her conduct, nor the vocabulary used to describe her suggests prostitution as her former trade. Long and flowing hair, especially among unmarried woman, suggests beauty and not shame. Her alabaster jar is a luxury item, and pouring out its ointment is a generous display of honor to Jesus. The scene demonstrates that the nature of her former sinfulness and even the fact that she had been a sinner are now irrelevant, except to Simon, who is unable to understand. The woman has been forgiven, and, as the closing words of Jesus indicate, her faith has brought her salvation and peace (v. 50).

Jesus asked Simon, "Do you see this woman?" (v. 44). Jesus was able to see the woman as forgiven and changed, peaceful and saved, lovely and loving, but Simon was unable to truly "see" this woman. For those who have eyes to see, she can be seen as a model disciple. Her tears contrast with those of Peter, who wept bitterly after denying Jesus; her kisses contrast with the betraying kiss of Judas. She pours out the precious ointment out of love as Jesus poured out his costly blood for those he loves. The challenge for us is to be able to see the woman, not as a sinner but a lover, indeed to be able to see other women and men, as well as ourselves, as beloved and loving, transformed and reconciled, saved and redeemed by Jesus.

Meditatio

Use your imagination to meditate on this passage and allow it to change you.

‡ Reflecting on this passage, we can place ourselves in the scene and imagine the response of our sight, hearing, smell, taste, and touch. Which of the bodily sensations are most vivid to me? What does this scene teach me about the humanity of Jesus?

‡ How did Simon's prejudiced and stereotyped way of seeing prevent him from knowing this woman? What can I learn from Simon about seeing people truly?

‡ What prevents me from being more extravagant and lavish with my expressions of love?

Oratio

Pray to God from a heart that has been changed through your reflection on this passage.

> All-seeing God, you are able to see the hearts of your people and know the thoughts that are hidden from others. Gaze into my heart and transform me with knowledge of your forgiveness. Help me reflect the love you have shown to me and give me the vision to see others rightly.

Continue praying in whatever words arise from your heart . . .

Contemplatio

Imagine the mutual love of Jesus and the woman at his feet. Relax, knowing that Jesus sees your heart, and try to experience the love of Jesus for you.

Write a few words describing your contemplative experience of love.

Operatio

What would help me to see others as Jesus sees them? Which prejudices and stereotypes do I want to remove from my heart?

15

The Women Who Accompany Jesus

Lectio

Close off the distractions of the day and enter a still moment. Read this text aloud so that you hear the words and listen to the inspired passage.

LUKE 8:1–3

> [1]Soon afterwards he went on through cities and villages, proclaiming and bringing the good news of the kingdom of God. The twelve were with him, [2]as well as some women who had been cured of evil spirits and infirmities: Mary, called Magdalene, from whom seven demons had gone out, [3]and Joanna, the wife of Herod's steward Chuza, and Susanna, and many others, who provided for them out of their resources.

Continue exploring the implications of this brief passage for the church and the life of disciples everywhere.

All four of the Gospels indicate that Jesus had women disciples who followed him from Galilee to Jerusalem. Whereas Mark, Matthew, and John note the presence of these women at the crucifixion of Jesus, Luke is the only Gospel to document their presence with Jesus during his mission in

Galilee. While Jesus traveled through the cities and villages, bringing the Good News of God's kingdom, he was accompanied by "the twelve" as well as "some women who had been cured of evil spirits and infirmities" (v. 2). The casting out of evil spirits is often linked in Luke's Gospel with the healing of physical and mental disorders. Like many of Jesus's disciples, these women had experienced healing and compassion from Jesus, enabling them to become instruments of healing and compassion for others.

Mary Magdalene is always named first when she is associated with other women disciples, similar to the way Peter is always listed first among the male disciples. This is probably due to her more significant role or position of leadership among the women. We can assume that Mary Magdalene has neither a husband nor a son, since she would probably have been identified in relationship to one of them, as are most of the other women of the Gospels. Instead, she is associated with a city called Magdala, an important commercial center with a harbor and shipyards on the Sea of Galilee. Here fish were salted and processed for export. Mary may very well have been a businesswoman of Magdala's fishing industry.

Luke asserts that "seven demons had gone out" of Mary Magdalene. Demons could refer to any number of unexplainable symptoms: mental illness, erratic behavior, addictive desires, or satanic possession. The statement that there were seven demons signifies the intensity and chronic nature of her illness. There is no evidence in the Gospels that she was a prostitute or a public sinner, as she is commonly depicted in other media. Later writers most likely confused the unnamed sinner who anointed Jesus, whose scene immediately precedes this scene in Luke's Gospel, with Mary Magdalene. Jesus liberated Mary from her demons, enabling her to resocialize with the community, and she spent her life following him with gratitude. Her devotion and loyalty to Jesus are without parallel among his disciples.

Joanna was married to Chuza, who managed the vast estates of land owned by Galilee's ruler, Herod Antipas. Chuza had a position that generated considerable wealth and influence. Joanna and Chuza likely lived in Tiberias, the city Herod built for himself on the western shore of the Sea of Galilee, about three miles south of Magdala. The news of Jesus's preaching and healing had reached the court of Herod, undoubtedly generating a variety of responses. Some feared Jesus, like Herod, who thought he was

John the Baptist come back from the dead. Others were attracted to him, like Joanna, who became his disciple.

Susanna is not mentioned anywhere else in the Gospels, so we have no other information about her. Along with Mary, Joanna, and Susanna, Luke tells us there were "many others." There were many women who, along with the twelve male disciples, followed Jesus through the town of Galilee and then to the city of Jerusalem. It is possible that these three named women correspond with the inner circle of three men closest to Jesus: Peter, James, and John.

There are many unanswered questions about these women disciples from Galilee. We don't know their relationship to Jesus and to the male disciples. We don't know how they were looked upon by others in Jewish society for traveling with Jesus and the twelve. Luke tells us that they provided for Jesus and the band of disciples "out of their resources" (v. 3). This could certainly mean that the women supported the group with meals, clothing, and other domestic services, as the passage has been traditionally interpreted. More likely, however, "resources" refers to their money, property, goods, or possessions. Inscriptions found in synagogues of the time indicate that at least some women had means and assets and the power to donate them. These women supported Jesus and his other followers as financial patrons as well as disciples.

The women in this narrative had turned to Jesus in their need and had taken the risk to follow him. They had left behind the comforts of their status and now supported Jesus and his mission with their resources. In the eyes of others, they were Jesus's wealthy patrons. In their own eyes, they were his disciples, following him faithfully wherever their journey led.

See if you can answer these questions based on your study of the text:

✝ How might Mary Magdalene and Joanna have possessed wealth to support the mission of Jesus?

✝ Does the fact that Mary Magdalene is always listed first among the women disciples have any significance?

Meditatio

Imagine the traveling band of disciples moving with Jesus through the cities and villages of Galilee. Consider what they have to teach you about following Jesus.

✝ What does it mean to me that many women as well as men followed Jesus as disciples from Galilee to Jerusalem?

✝ Call aloud the names of Jesus's disciples: Peter, Mary Magdalene, James, Joanna, John, and Susanna. How does it influence my understanding of Jesus's mission to hear their names called out together?

✝ What risks would these wealthy women have taken in order to approach Jesus and follow in his way? What perils are faced by influential people today who decide to be disciples of Jesus?

Oratio

Respond to Jesus, who is transforming you through the Word as he transformed his disciples through his proclamation of the Good News.

Lord Jesus, you call your disciples to follow in your footsteps and to devote their lives to the mission of God's kingdom. Give me a burning desire to join the women and men of your company of disciples and to devote my life to the reign of God.

Continue voicing the prayer that issues from your heart . . .

Contemplatio

Listen to Jesus call your name within the list of his disciples. Take some time in quiet, preparing your heart to respond.

Write a few words reflecting on your call.

Operatio

In what way is my response to Jesus's call to discipleship continuing to change my life? How do Mary Magdalene, Joanna, and Susanna inspire me to follow more faithfully?

16

Martha and Mary Model
a Balanced Discipleship

Lectio

*Read the passage slowly and carefully, trying not to impose your precon-
ceived understanding on the text. Ask God's Spirit to help you read this familiar passage anew.*

LUKE 10:38–42

[38]Now as they went on their way, he entered a certain village, where
a woman named Martha welcomed him into her home. [39]She had a
sister named Mary, who sat at the Lord's feet and listened to what he
was saying. [40]But Martha was distracted by her many tasks; so she
came to him and asked, "Lord, do you not care that my sister has left
me to do all the work by myself? Tell her then to help me." [41]But the
Lord answered her, "Martha, Martha, you are worried and distracted
by many things; [42]there is need of only one thing. Mary has chosen
the better part, which will not be taken away from her."

*Continue listening for God's Word within this inspired text and discover its
fuller significance for the Christian life.*

This deceptively simple narrative is unique to Luke's Gospel, though Martha and Mary emerge again in John's Gospel with their brother, Lazarus. Traditionally this passage is interpreted as a contrast between the active and the contemplative life. Some recent interpreters see it as Luke's way of silencing women engaged in ministry. Others understand it as an opening to women, challenging traditional expectations about their roles. When Christian women ask themselves whether they are Martha or Mary, the passage reveals that both sisters can be models for a balanced discipleship. Both women and men can learn from this complex and controversial text how to hear the Word of God and do it. As the Gospel scene reveals its multiple layers of meaning, today's disciples can see their own service to the reign of God mirrored in these two sisters.

The traveling ministry of Jesus and his disciples certainly depended on the hospitality extended to them by people like Martha and Mary. The invitation of Martha was offered not only to Jesus but also to his whole entourage of male and female disciples. Martha and Mary were probably householders who managed a staff of servants within an extended family. Martha's welcome, however, meant not just preparing food and lodging for such a crowd. It expressed her embrace of Jesus's mission and her desire to contribute to it. But while Martha was busy seeing to the details of hospitality, Jesus was teaching in her own home and she didn't hear a word of it.

Her sister, Mary, in contrast, "sat at the Lord's feet and listened to what he was saying" (v. 39). In the rabbinic tradition of Judaism, sitting at the feet of a teacher was the position of devoted discipleship. There a disciple learned the teacher's wisdom, just as Paul learned "at the feet of Gamaliel" (Acts 22:3). Luke's writing enforces the importance of listening, of hearing the Word, and of learning from Jesus as essential characteristics of discipleship. Mary, then, is the perfect portrait of the listening disciple.

The contrast of Martha and Mary is not just between serving and listening. Martha is described as "distracted by her many tasks," stressed and agitated by all that she is doing (v. 40). This contrast is reinforced by the gentle reprimand of Jesus: "Martha, Martha, you are worried and distracted by many things" (v. 41). Martha's use of first-person pronouns in her speech continually refers back to herself: "Lord, do you not care that *my* sister has left *me* to do all the work by *myself*? Tell her then to help *me*." This self-centered concern contrasts with Mary's single-minded focus on the words of Jesus.

The embarrassing social situation and quarrel between the sisters set us up to carefully hear and ponder the climactic response of Jesus. In contrast to the "many things" of Martha, Jesus says, "There is need of only one thing. Mary has chosen the better part" (v. 42). In leaving her expected role of performing domestic tasks in order to listen to Jesus, Mary has taken a bold action. She is in the male part of the house rather than in the back rooms where the women usually worked. But it is a choice strongly defended by Jesus, who insists that it "will not be taken away from her." Because of examples like Mary, we find many women in positions of leadership, teaching, and responsibility in the early church.

Worry and anxiety are debilitating hindrances to effective discipleship. Jesus specifically warns his disciples not to be anxious: "Do not worry about your life, what you will eat, or about your body, what you will wear. . . . And can any of you by worrying add a single hour to your span of life?" (12:22–25). Instead, Jesus urges disciples to strive first for God's kingdom, and then everything else will be given as well. Martha's anxiety about many things distracts her from the one thing necessary. Centering her heart on Jesus is what Mary is doing so well.

The word for the many "tasks" of Martha is translated from the Greek word *diakonia*, which is translated elsewhere as "service" or "ministry." For this reason, we realize that Martha's work symbolizes more than kitchen-bound service for Jesus and his crew. The Gospel contrasts Martha and Mary in order to highlight the characteristics of Christian ministry and service within the church. The story is not addressed to women only but to all disciples. Its purpose is not to describe the ideal woman disciple but to deepen the understanding of discipleship for all readers.

In affirming the choice of Mary, we may feel that Martha's hospitality and service are devalued. Yet, when Jesus highlighted the one thing necessary, he did not mean that everything else has no importance. These sisters are not caricatures of two opposing choices, one of which must be selected over the other. This is not a contrast between a fussy, argumentative busybody and her tranquil, attentive sister. Rather, the sisters express two interdependent aspects of discipleship, both of which are necessary. Hearing the Word and doing it are both essential and complementary facets of following Jesus. There is a time to listen and a time to act.

Meditatio

Reflect on what is most surprising, instructive, and inspiring for you from the scene of the two sisters.

✝ In what ways do I see both Martha and Mary within my own discipleship? Which am I most comfortable with?

✝ How do I strike an appropriate balance between the hearing of Mary and the doing of Martha?

✝ What was Jesus trying to teach Martha? What lessons do I learn from this Gospel narrative?

Oratio

Interact with God, who knows you intimately, cares about you deeply, and accepts you unconditionally.

> Lord, in the midst of life's many tasks, help me to remember that "there is need of only one thing." Teach me to listen to your Word before I act upon it, and show me that your Word is the essential wellspring of all my service.

Continue praying to God, using the words and images of the text to respond to him . . .

Contemplatio

Mary is the model for contemplatio. In your mind, place yourself in the position of Mary, at the feet of Jesus. Just rest there and listen.

Write a few words summarizing your contemplative experience at the feet of Jesus.

Operatio

Martha is the model for operatio, representing the active disciple engaged in service. What have I learned about my ministry from both Martha and Mary?

17

A Woman in the Crowd Cries Out

Lectio

In a quiet and comfortable place, read the words of Scripture, seeking to understand their meaning.

LUKE 8:19–21

¹⁹Then his mother and his brothers came to him, but they could not reach him because of the crowd. ²⁰And he was told, "Your mother and your brothers are standing outside, wanting to see you." ²¹But he said to them, "My mother and my brothers are those who hear the word of God and do it."

LUKE 11:27–28

²⁷While he was saying this, a woman in the crowd raised her voice and said to him, "Blessed is the womb that bore you and the breasts that nursed you!" ²⁸But he said, "Blessed rather are those who hear the word of God and obey it!"

Continue to listen for the Word of God through the teaching and scholarship of the church.

In Luke's scene of the visit of Mary to her kinswoman, Elizabeth declares that the mother of Jesus is blessed because she bears Jesus in her womb (1:42) and because she believes the Word of God: "And blessed is she who believed that there would be a fulfillment of what was spoken to her by the Lord" (1:45). Thus, she praises Mary both as the "mother of my Lord" (1:43) and as an icon of Christian believers. Already in the opening scenes of his Gospel, Luke is emphasizing that biological ties are not the most important consideration in the new family of God that Jesus is establishing. Most important is believing God's Word and responding to that Word in obedience.

Luke places the scene with the biological family of Jesus immediately after his parable of the sower and uses the scene to illustrate its truth. The good soil represents those who hear the Word of God, hold it fast, and bear fruit. When the mother and brothers of Jesus come to see him, Jesus uses the occasion to teach that the family of God includes all who listen to God's Word and do it (8:21). Luke thus eliminates in his account of the scene the distance and tension that are present between Jesus and his biological family in Mark's Gospel. Luke has made it clear from the beginning that Jesus's mother hears and obeys God's Word and that the family is a model of faithfulness. Luke therefore is sure to include the family of Nazareth among the new family of God formed from obedient listening.

The natural family is a primary place of affection and the principle source of security in ancient culture. The woman who raised her voice in the crowd highlights this natural bond between mother and child by proclaiming, "Blessed is the womb that bore you and the breasts that nursed you!" (11:27). In response, Jesus transfers the primary family ties from the biological categories to a spiritual category. The primary criterion for being a part of the new family of Jesus is listening to God's Word and putting it into practice: "Blessed rather are those who hear the word of God and obey it!" (11:28). While the woman in the crowd attributes Mary's blessedness to her role as mother, Jesus emphasizes that blessedness does not lie only in the womb and the breasts but in responding with fidelity to the Word of God.

Luke's Gospel goes on to offer an even more radical critique of conventional family ties. The coming of Jesus creates the necessity of decision, which often brings division before it brings peace, even within households: "from now on five in one household will be divided, three against two and two against three; they will be divided: father against son and son against father, mother against daughter and daughter against mother, mother-in-law against her daughter-in-law and daughter-in-law against mother-in-law" (12:52–53). The harmony of the household is disrupted by the decision of discipleship. The biological bonds within families can no longer be the primary source of the identity and security of a disciple.

Jesus amplifies his point later in the Gospel, including more family members and even one's own life, in stating the radical demands of discipleship: "Whoever comes to me and does not hate father and mother, wife and children, brothers and sisters, yes, and even life itself, cannot be my disciple" (14:26). The saying underscores the preeminent place that Jesus must occupy in the life of anyone choosing to follow him. His forceful hyperbole makes it clear that one's love and loyalty to Jesus must outweigh all other allegiances. Yet, Jesus also assures his followers that their gains will far exceed their loss: "There is no one who has left house or wife or brothers or parents or children, for the sake of the kingdom of God, who will not get back very much more in this age, and in the age to come eternal life" (18:29–30). The division and loss that a disciple may experience are always for the sake of the kingdom of God.

Of course, following Jesus does not necessarily disband the biological family. Jesus's teachings on the permanency of marriage and the responsibilities of parents to children make that clear. Luke verifies that the mother of Jesus along with his brothers continued their discipleship into the life of the early church (Acts 1:14). Yet, as the family of Jesus demonstrates as well as any, the spiritual kinship formed between those who hear and obey God's Word is the permanent and most vital bond for God's kingdom in the world.

Meditatio

Spend some time reflecting on the text, asking yourself what personal message the passage has for you.

‡ What surprises me most about these verses? Do I take exception to any of them?

‡ What is the primary point Jesus wishes to make in his teachings on biological families and his new spiritual family?

‡ In what way does Jesus's description of family membership, "those who hear the word of God and do it" include Martha and Mary as well as his own mother?

Oratio

Using the ideas generated by the text, spend some time responding to God with words that flow from your reflection.

> God our Father, you invite us into your household to share in your family through the life of Jesus our brother. Help me to listen attentively and single-mindedly to the Word of God and to respond to it with dedication so that I may share in the new family of Jesus along with brothers and sisters throughout the world.

Continue responding to God with words generated by your reflection on the Scripture . . .

Contemplatio

Recall your most comforting and peaceful experience of family life. Recall the emotions of that moment and allow them to fill your heart, knowing that God wants you to share deeply in the joys of his family.

Write a brief note about your feelings during this time of contemplation.

Operatio

What have I learned about being a disciple of Jesus through this lectio divina today? How is God shaping my ability to live in his family as I reflectively read this passage?

18

The Crippled Woman Set Free from Bondage

Lectio

Kiss the words of Scripture, asking God to help you reverence the divine Word within. Be grateful for God's invitation to listen to Scripture.

LUKE 13:10–17

[10]Now he was teaching in one of the synagogues on the sabbath. [11]And just then there appeared a woman with a spirit that had crippled her for eighteen years. She was bent over and was quite unable to stand up straight. [12]When Jesus saw her, he called her over and said, "Woman, you are set free from your ailment." [13]When he laid his hands on her, immediately she stood up straight and began praising God. [14]But the leader of the synagogue, indignant because Jesus had cured on the sabbath, kept saying to the crowd, "There are six days on which work ought to be done; come on those days and be cured, and not on the sabbath day." [15]But the Lord answered him and said, "You hypocrites! Does not each of you on the sabbath untie his ox or his donkey from the manger, and lead it away to give it water? [16]And ought not this woman, a daughter of Abraham whom Satan bound for eighteen long years, be set free from this bondage on the sabbath day?" [17]When he said this, all his opponents were put to shame; and the entire crowd was rejoicing at all the wonderful things that he was doing.

After listening carefully to this healing narrative, continue seeking the meaning and significance of the text.

Luke's Gospel locates this scene along the journey of Jesus toward Jerusalem, the place of his destiny where Jesus will accomplish his "exodus" (in Luke 9:31, "departure" is a weak translation of the Greek work *exodus*). The Gospel associates the exodus of Jesus with Israel's liberation from bondage, the central event that formed Israel into God's people. As this woman is "set free from this bondage" (v. 16), she foreshadows the liberating deeds of Jesus to free all people from the shackles that bind them. Luke underscores this association with the exodus by referring to the saving deeds of Jesus as "wonderful things" (v. 17) a translation of the same term used in the Old Testament (Exod. 34:10; Deut. 10:21) to refer to the liberating action of God for Israel.

The woman was "bent over and was quite unable to stand up straight," an affliction so common in older people throughout the world today (v. 11). In addition to the pain of such a condition, this woman was never able to meet another person face-to-face, and her world was confined to the space around her own feet. Luke describes her condition as the result of a crippling spirit, an evil power that disfigures and diminishes human life. The saving deeds of Jesus rescue people from these malevolent forces that prevent people from living in the fullness and freedom that God intends. Her eighteen-year affliction parallels the eighteen years the Israelites were subjugated to Moab (Judg. 3:14) and the eighteen years of oppression by the Ammonites (Judg. 10:8). Yet, these many years of bondage have not trampled this woman's inner strength, for she has come to the synagogue to worship God.

Jesus has come to teach in the synagogue, as was his custom, on the Sabbath, an expression of God's ongoing commitment and faithfulness to the children of Abraham. When Jesus sees her, he interrupts his teaching and calls her into the center of the community, saying, "Woman, you are set free from your ailment" (v. 12). Liberated from her long bondage, she stands up straight and praises God.

The woman's praise and the crowd's rejoicing form a sharp contrast to the irritation of the religious official (v. 14). The synagogue leader should not be depicted as legalistic or small-minded for offering his interpretation of Sabbath observance. This is what the Torah commands: "Observe the Sabbath day and keep it holy, as the LORD your God commanded you. For six days you shall labor and do all your work. But the seventh day is a sabbath to the LORD your God; you shall not do any work—you, or your son or your daughter, or your male or female slave, or your ox or your donkey" (Deut. 5:12–14). Sabbath observance for Jews was profoundly important for maintaining their religious identity and cultural integrity. The official knew that the woman's affliction was chronic and not life-threatening. Surely Jesus could have chosen any other day or at least waited a few hours until sundown to heal this woman (v. 14).

In his engagement with the official, Jesus by no means questions the principle of Sabbath observance, for his very presence in the synagogue testifies to his commitment to it. What Jesus challenges is the application of Sabbath regulations, and using good rabbinical method, he argues from a lesser example to a greater. Since the Torah includes the ox and donkey in the Sabbath regulations, and since Jewish tradition allows an owner to release his ox or donkey to get water on the Sabbath, then surely it would be even more fitting to release this daughter of Abraham from her long bondage (vv. 15–16).

In setting this woman free, Jesus highlights the very essence of the Sabbath as a remembrance of Israel's exodus from slavery, for the same Torah regulation continues, "Remember that you were a slave in the land of Egypt, and the LORD your God brought you out from there with a mighty hand and an outstretched arm; therefore the LORD your God commanded you to keep the sabbath day" (Deut 5:15). In laying his outstretched hands on the woman, Jesus makes the Sabbath truly holy, bringing her the freedom that God wants for all his people.

After hearing the words of this text, try to answer the following questions:

‡ Why does Luke relate this account to Israel's exodus from slavery?

‡ Does Jesus violate the Sabbath or honor it with this healing?

Meditatio

Spend some time meditating on this healing narrative in the context of God's overall saving plan from ancient times and into your own life.

✝ Why is the Sabbath the most appropriate day on which to free this woman? In what way does the release of this woman from bondage honor and make holy the Sabbath?

✝ One of the devastating effects of chronic illnesses is the way it ostracizes people from community. In what ways can my community welcome people with infirmities and disabilities?

✝ We can make a distinction between physical cures and more all-encompassing healing. In the absence of a cure, we can help people to heal by empathizing with their pain, supporting them in community, and surrounding their suffering with respect and love. How can I help in the healing process of others?

Oratio

Pray to God from your heart in whatever way seems to respond to the divine Word spoken to you through this Gospel text.

God of the exodus, you freed your people from endless labor by bringing them out of Egypt, and you established the Sabbath to honor human liberation. Free me from those things that diminish my life and help me to be an instrument of your freedom for others.

Continue praying using the biblical vocabulary you have heard . . .

Contemplatio

The Sabbath is God's way of sanctifying freedom and rest from labor. Spend a few moments of Sabbath time without thinking or doing but resting in the freedom God has given you.

Write a few words about your time of liberating rest.

Operatio

God desires us to be freed from endless striving through the grace of rest. How can I honor and make holy the freedom and leisure God gives to me?

19

The Mother of Jesus
Intercedes at the
Wedding Feast

Lectio

In your quiet space, light a candle, ring a chime, or kiss the text to prepare yourself to encounter the inspired Word. Vocalize the words of the text so that you not only read with your eyes but also hear with your ears.

JOHN 2:1–12

¹On the third day there was a wedding in Cana of Galilee, and the mother of Jesus was there. ²Jesus and his disciples had also been invited to the wedding. ³When the wine gave out, the mother of Jesus said to him, "They have no wine." ⁴And Jesus said to her, "Woman, what concern is that to you and to me? My hour has not yet come." ⁵His mother said to the servants, "Do whatever he tells you." ⁶Now standing there were six stone water jars for the Jewish rites of purification, each holding twenty or thirty gallons. ⁷Jesus said to them, "Fill the jars with water." And they filled them up to the brim. ⁸He said to them, "Now draw some out, and take it to the chief steward." So they took it. ⁹When the steward tasted the water that had become wine, and did not know where it came from (though the servants who had drawn the water knew), the steward

called the bridegroom ¹⁰and said to him, "Everyone serves the good wine first, and then the inferior wine after the guests have become drunk. But you have kept the good wine until now." ¹¹Jesus did this, the first of his signs, in Cana of Galilee, and revealed his glory; and his disciples believed in him.

¹²After this he went down to Capernaum with his mother, his brothers, and his disciples; and they remained there a few days.

After reading this account of the wedding at Cana, keep listening for its fullest meaning through this commentary.

The first person introduced in this wedding scene is "the mother of Jesus" (v. 1). She is accompanied at the celebration by Jesus and his disciples, and she initiates the action of the scene with her statement to Jesus, "They have no wine" (v. 3). Following what seems to be a sharp response from her son, she determinedly instructs the waiter, "Do whatever he tells you" (v. 5). Her words initiate a series of events that lead to the miracle and confidently teach the waiters as well as all the readers of John's Gospel that they should put into action whatever Jesus tells them to do. She is the first person in the Gospel to show that the appropriate response to the presence of Jesus is trusting obedience to his word. Even in the face of seeming rebuke, the mother of Jesus trusts unreservedly in the efficacy of the words of Jesus, becoming in this opening miracle of the Gospel the model of a true believer and disciple.

The response of Jesus to his mother's words sets up a tension in the account that will be resolved at the end of the Gospel. Jesus addresses her as "woman," an indication that her function in the Gospel is not just that of Jesus's earthly mother. She also has a more representative role. Jesus's words to her, "My hour has not yet come" (v. 4) anticipates the future glorification of Jesus on the cross. This initial scene looks forward to the completion of that "hour" of Jesus. The faith of the "woman" begins a series of events that will lead to that climactic glorification. At the cross, the mother of Jesus, the woman, will return, becoming then the mother of his disciples (19:26–27). In this way, the transformation of the water into wine, "the first of his signs" (v. 11), becomes a foreshadowing of the transformation yet to come. The miracle "revealed his glory," a glimpse of the glory that will be fully revealed when Jesus is lifted up on the cross.

Throughout the Mediterranean world, a miraculous gift of wine was associated with the presence of a deity, especially the god Dionysos. The writings of Israel's prophets spoke of abundant wine as an expression of the Messiah's coming: "The mountains shall drip sweet wine, and all the hills shall flow with it" (Amos 9:13). In those future days, God would provide for all people a banquet of rich food and "a feast of well-aged wines" (Isa. 25:6). At the wedding feast of Cana, the six huge jars were filled "up to the brim" (vv. 6–7). This is no cautious allotment for the guests. The results were well over a hundred gallons of fine wine.

Later in John's Gospel, Jesus reveals that he came into the world so that people may experience life bountifully: "I came that they may have life, and have it abundantly" (10:10). The miracle of abundant wine signals the unlimited possibility that Jesus brings to the world. Never again would life be as predictable, bland, and colorless as water; life in Jesus becomes rich, vibrant, and luscious. Jesus came to show people the abundant life for which they have always longed.

After tasting "the water that had become wine," the chief steward of the wedding feast called the bridegroom and said, "You have kept the good wine until now" (v. 10). The "now" is the time awaited by the prophets, the time of fulfillment, the beginning of the Messiah's mission. The miracle of the abundant wine is the first "sign" of the incarnate Word in the world, the first of seven "signs" in John's Gospel leading to the great sign of the cross. The instructions of the mother of Jesus to the servants, "Do whatever he tells you" (v. 5) are followed to perfection at the wedding feast. She continues to instruct disciples in every age to trust expectantly in the Word of her son, Jesus.

Try to answer this question after listening to the text and reading its commentary:

‡ Why doesn't John's Gospel call the mother of Jesus by her given name, Mary?

Meditatio

Imagine the sights, sounds, tastes, and smells of this scene of the wedding at Cana. Repeat and ponder whatever words or phrases strike you from your reading.

✠ The mother of Jesus says, "Do whatever he tells you." What does this instruction tell me about trust, expectancy, and obedience?

✠ What characteristics of wine express the quality of divine life present in Jesus? How is my ordinary life transformed because of him?

✠ In what way does John's Gospel present Mary as both mother and disciple of Jesus? In which role is she most inspiring to me?

Oratio

Respond to the Gospel account of Jesus's first "sign" with your own prayer of praise and thanksgiving.

Lord Jesus, you turn water to wine and transform ordinary existence into abundant living. Thank you for manifesting the power of your goodness and for opening my eyes to see the signs of divine presence all around me.

Continue praying with a heart filled with gratitude...

Contemplatio

Imagine that the feasting and celebration of the wedding have ended and the crowd has returned home. Sit in silence and ponder the goodness of God that you have just experienced.

Write a few words from your silent contemplation.

Operatio

What would help me to see the vibrant, abundant possibilities within the ordinary, predictable elements of my life? How can I adjust my vision?

20

The Woman of Samaria
Encounters Jesus

Listen carefully to this conversation between Jesus and the Samaritan woman.
Note any words or phrases that strike you in a new way in this familiar text.

JOHN 4:3–26

³[Jesus] left Judea and started back to Galilee. ⁴But he had to go
through Samaria. ⁵So he came to a Samaritan city called Sychar, near
the plot of ground that Jacob had given to his son Joseph. ⁶Jacob's
well was there, and Jesus, tired out by his journey, was sitting by the
well. It was about noon.

⁷A Samaritan woman came to draw water, and Jesus said to her,
"Give me a drink." ⁸(His disciples had gone to the city to buy food.)
⁹The Samaritan woman said to him, "How is it that you, a Jew, ask
a drink of me, a woman of Samaria?" (Jews do not share things in
common with Samaritans.) ¹⁰Jesus answered her, "If you knew the
gift of God, and who it is that is saying to you, 'Give me a drink,' you
would have asked him, and he would have given you living water."
¹¹The woman said to him, "Sir, you have no bucket, and the well is
deep. Where do you get that living water? ¹²Are you greater than our

ancestor Jacob, who gave us the well, and with his sons and his flocks drank from it?" [13]Jesus said to her, "Everyone who drinks of this water will be thirsty again, [14]but those who drink of the water that I will give them will never be thirsty. The water that I will give will become in them a spring of water gushing up to eternal life." [15]The woman said to him, "Sir, give me this water, so that I may never be thirsty or have to keep coming here to draw water."

[16]Jesus said to her, "Go, call your husband, and come back." [17]The woman answered him, "I have no husband." Jesus said to her, "You are right in saying, 'I have no husband'; [18]for you have had five husbands, and the one you have now is not your husband. What you have said is true!" [19]The woman said to him, "Sir, I see that you are a prophet. [20]Our ancestors worshiped on this mountain, but you say that the place where people must worship is in Jerusalem." [21]Jesus said to her, "Woman, believe me, the hour is coming when you will worship the Father neither on this mountain nor in Jerusalem. [22]You worship what you do not know; we worship what we know, for salvation is from the Jews. [23]But the hour is coming, and is now here, when the true worshipers will worship the Father in spirit and truth, for the Father seeks such as these to worship him. [24]God is spirit, and those who worship him must worship in spirit and truth." [25]The woman said to him, "I know that Messiah is coming" (who is called Christ). "When he comes, he will proclaim all things to us." [26]Jesus said to her, "I am he, the one who is speaking to you."

Continue listening to the text for its full meaning and significance.

The well was the center of life for the people of the Bible. It tapped into ground water, and so in the dry summers it was their source of life-sustaining water. It was also a gathering place, a place where people met for conversation and laughter. It was even a place where love began. It was at a well that Jacob met Rachel and Moses met Zipporah. So when Jesus meets the Samaritan woman at the well of Jacob, we should be prepared for an encounter filled with profound possibility.

The woman is shocked that Jesus should speak to her (v. 9). A Jewish man of the time would ordinarily not speak to an unknown woman alone, and generally the Jews ignored if not detested the Samaritans. Jesus did not plead ignorance; he was fully aware of the social rules and the Jewish intolerance of Samaritans. Yet, Jesus frequently broke social and religious boundaries for a higher good. Here Jesus uses his physical thirst as the occasion to address the deeper thirst of the Samaritan woman.

Jesus responds that if the woman knew who he was, she would have asked him for a drink—and he would have given her not well water but "living water" (v. 10). On the natural level, living water is flowing water, the water of a spring that is always fresh and sparkling. But the real contrast is between the well water of ordinary existence and the living water of abundant life in God's Spirit (vv. 13–14). The woman begins to realize that Jesus is offering her far more than water. He wants to bestow upon her a new kind of life, a life that begins with forgiveness and baptism then extends into eternal life.

Jesus's prophetic insight about the Samaritan woman's marital state is usually interpreted as his attempt to get the woman to acknowledge her sinful past in order to receive the new life he is offering her. The woman admits that she has no husband, and Jesus acknowledges that she is correct, for she has had five husbands, and the one with her now is not her husband (vv. 17–18). While this might describe a tragic marital history, there is another possible interpretation of this text. The book of 2 Kings describes the resettlement of Samaria after the Assyrian conquest. People from five foreign nations settled there and mixed with the remaining people of Israel. Each of these peoples brought their own gods and religious practices, which compromised the covenant faith of Israel (2 Kings 17:24, 29–34). If the five husbands symbolized Samaria's relationships with these five idolatrous peoples, then the sixth, or present liaison, would be the Samaritans' infidelity to God by their worship on Mount Gerazim.

This interpretation seems probable in light of the Samaritan woman's response to Jesus, which has nothing to do with marriage but is concerned with the correct place for worshipping God. The Samaritans considered Mount Gerizim the proper place of sacrifice, while the Jews held Jerusalem to be the only suitable place (v. 20). Jesus replies that the place of worship will be relatively unimportant at the coming of the Messiah, when believers will worship in spirit and in truth (v. 24).

Meditatio

After considering the interpretive commentary on this narrative, ask yourself what it says and means to you.

‡ Jesus frequently crossed boundaries that divided people in order to show that God's grace is available to all people. What does Jesus's encounter with the Samaritan woman teach me about God's favor and work in the world?

‡ According to the interpretation offered here, the woman represents the Samaritan people, and the whole encounter at the well expresses the wooing of Samaria to complete fidelity with God through the new covenant in Jesus. What idols or practices distract my worship of God in spirit and truth? How might God want to renew my worship?

‡ The Samaritan woman asks for the living water that Jesus offers. In what way does living water express the kind of life that Jesus gives to me?

Oratio

After listening to Jesus's dialogue with the Samaritan woman and considering its meaning, respond to Jesus by expressing the thoughts and feelings that arise from your heart.

> Source of living water, help me to realize my thirst for you and for the new life you offer me. Quench my thirst with the gift of your Spirit and renew the grace of baptism within me. May I praise you in the Spirit and seek your truth.

Continue pouring out your prayer until words are no longer necessary or useful...

Contemplatio

In a quiet and restful place, ask God to bathe you with the waters of renewing life and to refresh you with the living water of the Spirit.

Write a few words about your time of spiritual refreshment.

Operatio

The text tells us that Jesus "had to go through Samaria," even though most Jews went around Samaria on their way from Jerusalem to Galilee. What boundaries do I need to cross today in order to live up to my Christian mission?

21

The Samaritan Woman Witnesses to Jesus

Lectio

Continue reading this account of Jesus and the Samaritan woman. Enter the heart of Jesus and the woman through the sacred text.

JOHN 4:27–42

[27]Just then his disciples came. They were astonished that he was speaking with a woman, but no one said, "What do you want?" or, "Why are you speaking with her?" [28]Then the woman left her water jar and went back to the city. She said to the people, [29]"Come and see a man who told me everything I have ever done! He cannot be the Messiah, can he?" [30]They left the city and were on their way to him. [31]Meanwhile the disciples were urging him, "Rabbi, eat something." [32]But he said to them, "I have food to eat that you do not know about." [33]So the disciples said to one another, "Surely no one has brought him something to eat?" [34]Jesus said to them, "My food is to do the will of him who sent me and to complete his work. [35]Do you not say, 'Four months more, then comes the harvest'? But I tell you, look around you, and see how the fields are ripe for harvesting. [36]The reaper is already receiving wages and is gathering fruit for eternal life, so that sower and reaper may rejoice together. [37]For here the saying holds true,

'One sows and another reaps.' ³⁸I sent you to reap that for which you did not labor. Others have labored, and you have entered into their labor." ³⁹Many Samaritans from that city believed in him because of the woman's testimony, "He told me everything I have ever done." ⁴⁰So when the Samaritans came to him, they asked him to stay with them; and he stayed there two days. ⁴¹And many more believed because of his word. ⁴²They said to the woman, "It is no longer because of what you said that we believe, for we have heard for ourselves, and we know that this is truly the Savior of the world."

Enhance your understanding of this narrative through the interpretation offered here.

As the disciples return to Jesus, the Samaritan woman returns to her city. The contrast between the male disciples and the woman could not be greater. While the men are "astonished that he was speaking with a woman" (v. 27), this astonishing woman is going forth to witness to Jesus (vv. 28–29). While the men are occupied with eating the food they have bought, the woman is evangelizing the Samaritans. While the disciples are trying to understand why Jesus doesn't seem hungry (vv. 31–33), the Samaritans are already leaving their city to come to Jesus as a result of the woman's testimony (v. 30). Clearly this woman does the work of an apostle: proclaiming the Good News, witnessing to Jesus, and bringing others to him.

As the woman departs from the well to tell the Good News in the city, she leaves her water jar behind (v. 28). The Gospel writer's mention of the abandoned water jar is an intriguing detail. Perhaps it expresses the fact that she now possesses living water and will never thirst again (v. 14). Perhaps it conveys her haste and apostolic zeal to witness to Jesus. Most interestingly, many commentators see it as the feminine counterpart to the nets and boats the male disciples left behind to follow Jesus.

The Samaritan woman's style of evangelizing can be a refreshing model for our own. She has no certain answers, no prepackaged formulas she tries to impose on her listeners. Her witness is invitational. She encourages others to "come and see" what she herself has experienced in Jesus (v. 29). Her faith is still tentative and undeveloped. She is still full of questions: "He cannot be the Messiah, can he?" (v. 29). She invites others to share in her searching. She has come to believe first that Jesus is a prophet (v. 19), then the Messiah (vv. 25–26), and finally, along with increasingly more Samaritans, Savior of the world (v. 42). Though her belief is still hesitant and immature, she demonstrates an apostolic zeal, since it is impossible to keep such Good News to oneself.

While the disciples are urging Jesus to eat something, Jesus states that he is sustained and nourished by doing the work of the Father: "My food is to do the will of him who sent me and to complete his work" (v. 34). Likewise, the "daily bread" of those of us who follow him must be seeking to understand our mission and carrying out the work he has given us. Despite a balanced diet of physical food, we become malnourished unless we are sustained by a meaningful life in relationship to God. Jesus invites his disciples to the nourishing work of reaping the harvest that will result from what Jesus is sowing. Jesus, sent by the Father, in turn sends his disciples to continue his work (v. 38).

Jesus tells his disciples to look around and see the Samaritans coming to faith in him, like fields ripe for harvesting (v. 35). Though the Samaritans must have seemed to the Jews of the time unlikely prospects for salvation, the seeds of grace are sown in unlikely places and produce "fruit for eternal life" (v. 36). Many Samaritans came to believe in Jesus "because of the woman's testimony" (v. 39). Then, when they welcomed Jesus into their lives and spent time with him, "many more believed because of his word" (v. 41). They came to know and trust for themselves that Jesus is "truly the Savior of the world" (v. 42). God's purposes are being fulfilled: God sent his Son into the world "in order that the world might be saved through him" (3:17).

After listening carefully to John's description of this scene, answer these questions based on your hearing:

‡ What meaning might the woman's water jar convey in this story?

‡ In what way is doing God's will like eating nourishing food?

Meditatio

Reflect on the words of this narrative for your own life. Allow these words to give you encouragement and enthusiasm.

✢ What new insights have emerged from my engagement with the story of the Samaritan woman?

✢ The Samaritan woman is the most effective evangelizer in the whole Gospel. What does she have to teach disciples about witness and missionary endeavors?

✢ What nourishes and sustains my life? What is the "daily bread" for which I pray? What is the fruit I am called to reap for God in the world?

Oratio

Respond to God's Word to you with your own words to God. Speak from your heart in response to the insights you have received.

> Savior of the world, you nourish my life by calling me to participate in your mission. My work is fruitless unless it is also the work of your Father. May I rejoice with you when others come to believe in you.

Continue to express your hopes, desires, struggles, and commitment...

Contemplatio

Rest in silent stillness while God works within you. Use the image of the abandoned water jar as your focus of attention. Invite God to fill it or use it in any way he desires.

Write a few words about your experience of resting in God.

Operatio

Exhorted by God's Word, what renewed sense of mission have I received? How will my life be different after encountering Jesus and the Samaritan woman?

22

The Woman Judged
Forgiven by Jesus

Read this familiar account as if you were reading it for the first time. Disregard your predetermined ideas of what the text will say so that you can be open to the new insights and encouragement God is offering you.

JOHN 8:1–11

[1]Then each of them went home, while Jesus went to the Mount of Olives. [2]Early in the morning he came again to the temple. All the people came to him and he sat down and began to teach them. [3]The scribes and the Pharisees brought a woman who had been caught in adultery; and making her stand before all of them, [4]they said to him, "Teacher, this woman was caught in the very act of committing adultery. [5]Now in the law Moses commanded us to stone such women. Now what do you say?" [6]They said this to test him, so that they might have some charge to bring against him. Jesus bent down and wrote with his finger on the ground. [7]When they kept on questioning him, he straightened up and said to them, "Let anyone among you who is without sin be the first to throw a stone at her." [8]And once again he bent down and wrote on the ground. [9]When they heard it, they went

away, one by one, beginning with the elders; and Jesus was left alone with the woman standing before him. [10]Jesus straightened up and said to her, "Woman, where are they? Has no one condemned you?" [11]She said, "No one, sir." And Jesus said, "Neither do I condemn you. Go your way, and from now on do not sin again."

Continue struggling to understand the full implications of this Scripture through reading these remarks.

The religious authorities clearly have no real concern for the fate of this woman. They are out to get Jesus. Neither do they care about the injured husband or the partner in adultery, who has apparently gotten off scot-free. They are testing Jesus in order to trap him so that they can bring a charge against him. The woman seems to be merely a prop in the scene, exhibit A at the trial. The backdrop of the scene is the temple, where Jesus has been teaching a large group of people. The setting is a public forum where the opponents of Jesus try to catch him in a conflict with the Torah of Israel.

The usual commentary on this scene focuses on the woman and issues of sexual sin. But the text demonstrates that those who are motivated by judgmental attitudes, wishing to condemn the woman, are equally the focus of the narrative. The Gospel writer unfolds this story in two parallel scenes, each beginning when Jesus bends down and writes on the ground (vv. 6, 8). Each time he rises from the ground, he pronounces a pivotal verse of the narrative. He speaks first to the scribes and Pharisees about sin (v. 7) and then to the woman about sin (vv. 10–11).

The woman's accusers state that she has been "caught in the very act of committing adultery" (v. 4). If so, then where is the man who was caught with the woman? The law of Moses, to which the accusers refer, prescribes the death penalty for both the man and the woman involved (Lev. 20:10; Deut. 22:22–24). Is this then an example of the persistent double standard applied to women's sexuality? Or does this indicate perhaps that the woman has been entrapped? Clearly concern for the woman is not the issue for these men.

In the midst of this awkward scene in which the religious authorities are hoping to put Jesus in a trap, Jesus responds calmly and tenderly. His first response is nonverbal; he bends down and writes with his finger on the ground. If nothing else can be made of this gesture, at least it buys time for reflection and separates Jesus from the zealous fervor of the woman's accusers. By lowering himself to the ground, Jesus physically distinguishes his position from theirs. Since this is the only time in the New Testament when Jesus is presented as writing, commentators have been perhaps overly concerned to know what he is communicating. Some have suggested that Jesus is writing out the sins of his opponents; others suggest that he is simply doodling in the dust, a sign of humanity's common origin and destiny (Gen. 3:19).

With tranquil confidence, in contrast to the pressurized hysteria of the scene, Jesus stands up and states, "Let anyone among you who is without sin be the first to throw a stone at her" (v. 7). The mob is disarmed. The accusers become the accused. They are forced to direct their gaze inward, where they are able to discern whether they are in a position to condemn the woman. To their credit, not one of them exempts himself from self-judgment and throws the first stone at her. As Jesus again stoops to the ground and writes in the dirt, his opponents gradually walk away. Though they had arrived on the scene as an undifferentiated rabble, they go away "one by one" (v. 9), as individuals who have become more aware of their inner selves through their encounter with Jesus.

Jesus is left alone with the woman. He again rises from the ground and speaks, this time to her. He is the first person to address her directly in the narrative. She is no longer an objectified exhibit at a trial but a genuine person. The forgiveness of Jesus gives her the opportunity to live her life anew. Not only has Jesus saved her physical life from those who would stone her, but he also refuses to let her be defined by the guilt of past sin and directs her toward a life of freedom with an open future in relationship to God.

In this parallel narrative, Jesus addresses both the religious authorities and the adulterous woman about the reality of sin. Both are invited to give up their old ways—to be healed from a spirit disfigured by judgmentalism and a marriage scarred by infidelity respectively. Jesus has taught that God did not send his Son into the world to "condemn" but so that the world might be "saved" (3:17). He wants us to be freed from our past and to experience God's transforming grace.

Meditatio

Read the Gospel text again, focusing on your new understanding of the text and seeking to appreciate how it impacts your own understanding of Jesus.

‡ In what way does this scene demonstrate Jesus's delicate balance between the justice of not condoning the sin and the mercy of forgiving sinners?

‡ From what types of imprisonment does Jesus free both the woman and the religious officials? In what way does judgmentalism provide the fuel for racism, sexism, and neglect of the poor?

‡ How does cultivating our ability to see ourselves as sinners enable us to extend ourselves in compassion to others?

Oratio

Offer your prayer to God with the words, ideas, and images from your experience of the Scripture.

> Just and merciful Lord, you forgave the sinful woman and the judgmental men. Help me to realize the depths of my sin and the liberation you offer me through your forgiveness. Continue to transform my life with your healing grace.

Continue to pray as your heart directs you . . .

Contemplatio

Be still before God, conscious of your sin and asking for the freedom of new life. Let God move your heart with compassion for yourself and others.

Write a few words about your contemplative experience.

Operatio

What can I do to be healed of a judgmental spirit? How can I cultivate a spirit of compassion?

23

Martha Expresses
Confidence in Jesus

*As you study this text and commentary, highlight or underline the parts you
wish to remember and return to for reflection. Let the Holy Spirit guide your
careful reading.*

JOHN 11:1–27

¹Now a certain man was ill, Lazarus of Bethany, the village of Mary
and her sister Martha. ²Mary was the one who anointed the Lord with
perfume and wiped his feet with her hair; her brother Lazarus was
ill. ³So the sisters sent a message to Jesus, "Lord, he whom you love
is ill." ⁴But when Jesus heard it, he said, "This illness does not lead
to death; rather it is for God's glory, so that the Son of God may be
glorified through it." ⁵Accordingly, though Jesus loved Martha and
her sister and Lazarus, ⁶after having heard that Lazarus was ill, he
stayed two days longer in the place where he was.
⁷Then after this he said to the disciples, "Let us go to Judea again."
⁸The disciples said to him, "Rabbi, the Jews were just now trying to
stone you, and are you going there again?" ⁹Jesus answered, "Are
there not twelve hours of daylight? Those who walk during the day

do not stumble, because they see the light of this world. ¹⁰But those who walk at night stumble, because the light is not in them." ¹¹After saying this, he told them, "Our friend Lazarus has fallen asleep, but I am going there to awaken him." ¹²The disciples said to him, "Lord, if he has fallen asleep, he will be all right." ¹³Jesus, however, had been speaking about his death, but they thought that he was referring merely to sleep. ¹⁴Then Jesus told them plainly, "Lazarus is dead. ¹⁵For your sake I am glad I was not there, so that you may believe. But let us go to him." ¹⁶Thomas, who was called the Twin, said to his fellow disciples, "Let us also go, that we may die with him."

¹⁷When Jesus arrived, he found that Lazarus had already been in the tomb four days. ¹⁸Now Bethany was near Jerusalem, some two miles away, ¹⁹and many of the Jews had come to Martha and Mary to console them about their brother. ²⁰When Martha heard that Jesus was coming, she went and met him, while Mary stayed at home. ²¹Martha said to Jesus, "Lord, if you had been here, my brother would not have died. ²²But even now I know that God will give you whatever you ask of him." ²³Jesus said to her, "Your brother will rise again." ²⁴Martha said to him, "I know that he will rise again in the resurrection on the last day." ²⁵Jesus said to her, "I am the resurrection and the life. Those who believe in me, even though they die, will live, ²⁶and everyone who lives and believes in me will never die. Do you believe this?" ²⁷She said to him, "Yes, Lord, I believe that you are the Messiah, the Son of God, the one coming into the world."

After reading this inspired narrative, continue listening for God's Word and seeking a deeper understanding.

John's Gospel tells us that Jesus is a dear friend of the two sisters, Martha and Mary, and their brother, Lazarus. The writer assumes the reader is already familiar with these friends of Jesus from circulating traditions. Though this Gospel echoes some of the characterizations of these two sisters from Luke's Gospel, it does not demonstrate any tension between the two sisters as seen in the other Gospel. Here, both Martha and Mary are in a state of crisis, and together they send a message to Jesus to tell him that his beloved friend is ill (v. 3). Even though Jesus loves the three members of this family, they receive no timely answer to their plea for help (vv. 5–6).

When Jesus does finally arrive in Bethany, Lazarus has already been in the tomb for several days. Many have come to console the two sisters over the death of their brother. As the account unfolds, Martha and Mary present two faces of grief, serving as inspirations and models for Christians reading the Gospel who face their own bereavement.

Martha is the first to come to meet Jesus, while Mary stays at home (v. 20). Remaining fairly composed, Martha demonstrates trust in Jesus. She is shown to be the model of confident faith in the midst of grief. Though her initial greeting might strike us as a reprimand of Jesus for delaying too long, "Lord, if you had been here, my brother would not have died," she follows with a statement of confidence. Even though her brother has died, she says, "But even now I know that God will give you whatever you ask of him" (vv. 21–22).

The response of Jesus, "Your brother will rise again," is ambiguous because he does not say when Lazarus will rise. His words seem to Martha only a pious consolation expressing the common Jewish belief that the just will rise again in the resurrection on the last day (vv. 23–24). Like the common Christian sentiment at funerals, "He's in a better place now," it doesn't cut the grief of the moment. But Jesus has much more in mind.

Jesus brings together Martha's faith in the future resurrection and her present trust in him by saying, "I am the resurrection and the life." He transforms her hope from a future expectation to a present experience. Jesus is, first, our resurrection: "Those who believe in me, even though they die, will live" (v. 25). For those united with Jesus through faith, death will not cut them off from the life God gives, and God will raise them up on the last day. Jesus is, second, our life: "Everyone who lives and believes in me will never die" (v. 26). The eternal life that we begin to experience now through faith in Jesus will never be extinguished, not even by death. Union with Jesus brings eternal life in the present; resurrection on the last day will bring that life to its fullness. Resurrection and eternal life are the fruit of a relationship with Jesus, so wherever Jesus is, there is life that never ends and the certain hope of resurrection.

Jesus asks Martha, "Do you believe this?" (v. 26). Martha replies with one of the great professions of faith in the Gospel (v. 27). Even before she witnesses the raising of Lazarus, Martha becomes as an exemplar of belief for all future Gospel readers.

Meditatio

Spend some time reflecting on those verses and sentences you highlighted during your lectio. Use your insights to respond to the following questions:

✝ What thoughts and emotions do I experience when contemplating the reality of death?

✝ What do I believe about the connection between my relationship with Jesus and my eternal destiny? In what way can deepening my faith in Jesus decrease my fear of death?

✝ How would I answer Jesus's question in verse 26? How can Martha's belief be a help to increase my own faith?

Oratio

In response to God's speaking to you through Scripture, bring your questions, fears, trust, and confidence to him in prayer.

Jesus, you are the resurrection and the life, the source of unending and glorious life forever. As I reflect on the reality of inevitable death, set me free from fear and anxiety. Help me to believe in you and entrust my future to you.

Continue this prayer in words that issue from your heart . . .

Contemplatio

When words are no longer helpful, just rest in God's presence with trusting confidence. Realize that God is transforming you from within through the gift of faith that now fills your heart.

Write a few words about your contemplative experience.

Operatio

What has Martha taught me about faith in the midst of grief? In what way do I want to imitate her trust?

24

Mary Weeps at the
Feet of Jesus

Put away the distractions of the day and enter a quiet place where you can hear God's voice speaking to you through the words of Scripture. Ask the Holy Spirit to fill your heart as you read.

JOHN 11:28–45

28When she had said this, she went back and called her sister Mary, and told her privately, "The Teacher is here and is calling for you." 29And when she heard it, she got up quickly and went to him. 30Now Jesus had not yet come to the village, but was still at the place where Martha had met him. 31The Jews who were with her in the house, consoling her, saw Mary get up quickly and go out. They followed her because they thought that she was going to the tomb to weep there. 32When Mary came where Jesus was and saw him, she knelt at his feet and said to him, "Lord, if you had been here, my brother would not have died."

33When Jesus saw her weeping, and the Jews who came with her also weeping, he was greatly disturbed in spirit and deeply moved. 34He said, "Where have you laid him?" They said to him, "Lord, come and see." 35Jesus began to weep. 36So the Jews said, "See how he loved him!" [37]But some of them said, "Could not he who opened the eyes of the blind man have kept this man from dying?"

[38]Then Jesus, again greatly disturbed, came to the tomb. It was a cave, and a stone was lying against it. [39]Jesus said, "Take away the stone." Martha, the sister of the dead man, said to him, "Lord, already there is a stench because he has been dead four days." [40]Jesus said to her, "Did I not tell you that if you believed, you would see the glory of God?" [41]So they took away the stone. And Jesus looked upward and said, "Father, I thank you for having heard me. [42]I knew that you always hear me, but I have said this for the sake of the crowd standing here, so that they may believe that you sent me." [43]When he had said this, he cried with a loud voice, "Lazarus, come out!" [44]The dead man came out, his hands and feet bound with strips of cloth, and his face wrapped in a cloth. Jesus said to them, "Unbind him, and let him go."

[45]Many of the Jews therefore, who had come with Mary and had seen what Jesus did, believed in him.

Continue searching for the fuller implications of this text through the commentary.

Mary had stayed at home in mourning while Martha went to see Jesus when he arrived in Bethany. But when Martha returns and summons her, Mary arises quickly and goes out to meet Jesus (v. 29). She presents a different face of grief than her sister. Mary immediately falls at the feet of Jesus and weeps (vv. 32–33). She repeats the same words as her sister, "Lord, if you had been here, my brother would not have died." Yet, because she does not add Martha's words of confidence, Mary's words seem to chastise Jesus for his delay. While Martha's grief was expressed with composed and confident trust, Mary's grief is expressed with emotional outpouring and tears.

The response of Jesus to Martha and Mary corresponds to the quite different situation of each woman. Responding to Martha's own trust in Jesus, he had offered a statement of faith, an expression of his own identity as the source of resurrection and life. In response to Mary's kneeling at his feet, Jesus expresses deep emotional involvement (vv. 33, 35). The emotional response of Jesus suggests a mixture of deep grief and profound anger at the great enemy, death, and what death has done to his friends Lazarus, Martha, and Mary. The verbal response that Jesus offered Martha and the emotional response he offers Mary represent two necessary and complementary aspects of faith: the response of the mind and the response of the heart. Each of them serves as consolation for Christians reading the Gospel who face the death of loved ones and their own grief.

The narrative of the raising of Lazarus is told briefly but powerfully. Jesus is weeping like Mary yet trusting like Martha. When Jesus commands, "Take away the stone," Martha expresses her practical humanity, warning of the stench and the foulness of death after four days in the tomb (v. 39). Jesus then renews his promise to her that she will see "the glory of God" (v. 40).

As Jesus prays, he knows that his petitions will be answered and that Lazarus will come to life. When Jesus calls Lazarus by name, the dead man emerges from the tomb, "his hands and feet bound with strips of cloth, and his face wrapped in a cloth" (v. 44). His bound condition reminds us that the resuscitation of Lazarus is far different from the resurrection of Jesus. Lazarus is raised from death only to die again. Jesus, the resurrection and the life, will leave the funeral wrappings in the tomb and emerge in total freedom to a new kind of life (20:6–7).

The command of Jesus, "Unbind him, and let him go" (v. 44), echoes the command spoken by Moses in the name of God: "Let my people go" (Exod. 5:1). God wants his people to be free from all bondage, even the final prison of death, so that they can experience the fullness of his eternal life. Like the exodus from Egypt, the raising of Lazarus is a sign and foreshadowing of what God will do for Jesus and for all who belong to him.

Try to answer this question based on the account of Martha, Mary, and Lazarus:

✝ What are the different ways that Martha and Mary respond in the face of their brother's death?

Meditatio

Bringing God's Word into the present context of your life, spend some time reflecting on these questions.

‡ In what ways is my response to death like that of Martha and Mary?

‡ What are the similarities and differences between the way that Martha and Mary are portrayed in the Gospel of Luke and their characterization in the Gospel of John?

‡ How does Mary's emotional response bring out the expression of Jesus's feelings over the death of his friend? How do the emotions of Jesus endear him to me?

Oratio

Martha and Mary teach us how to express our thoughts, desires, frustrations, and fears to Jesus. Forget about being somber and reserved before the One who knows you intimately and accepts you unconditionally.

Jesus, you are the resurrection and the life, the source of my hope and confidence in the future. You wept at the death of your friend Lazarus, and you passionately desire to set me free from fear and death. Assure me of your presence when I grieve life's losses and when I rejoice in life's gifts.

Continue speaking to Jesus as your heart directs . . .

Contemplatio

Place yourself in the presence of the One who gave you life and who will hold you firmly when earthly life departs. Trust that God will lead you always in the path of freedom and life.

Write a few words that arise from your contemplative experience of God's presence.

Operatio

What have I learned from Martha and Mary? How do I want to imitate their relationship with Jesus?

25

The Poor Widow Gives Everything

Lectio

Kiss the words of the biblical text and ask God to let these inspired words speak powerfully to your spirit today.

MARK 12:38–44

[38]As he taught, he said, "Beware of the scribes, who like to walk around in long robes, and to be greeted with respect in the marketplaces, [39]and to have the best seats in the synagogues and places of honor at banquets! [40]They devour widows' houses and for the sake of appearance say long prayers. They will receive the greater condemnation."

[41]He sat down opposite the treasury, and watched the crowd putting money into the treasury. Many rich people put in large sums. [42]A poor widow came and put in two small copper coins, which are worth a penny. [43]Then he called his disciples and said to them, "Truly I tell you, this poor widow has put in more than all those who are contributing to the treasury. [44]For all of them have contributed out of their abundance; but she out of her poverty has put in everything she had, all she had to live on."

After reading this passage with your mind and heart, continue listening to the inspired text through these comments.

The episode of the poor widow forms an overture to the Gospel's passion account. The woman gave "everything she had," literally "her whole life" (v. 44). This complete self-giving foreshadows the self-sacrifice that Jesus is about to make—the offering of his very life without reservation. The widow is one of several, often unnamed, female characters in the passion accounts who respond with greater faith than the twelve male disciples and thus serve as models for future disciples who read the Gospel.

As Jesus is teaching on the grounds of the temple, he offers two contrasting lessons on the appropriate behavior of a disciple. First, he warns against the conduct of the scribes who use their religious position to bring attention to themselves. They use the garments of their professional office as a means of obtaining public honors and privileges. In striking contrast to this hypocrisy, Jesus presents the example of the poor widow, who puts her two small coins into the temple treasury. Though the monetary value of her offering is insignificant, her gift represents total abandonment of herself to God. In contrast to the scribes, whose practice of religion is all show, she seeks to give honor to God with perfect surrender and trust.

Jesus watches as people put their monetary donations into the treasury—and probably listens as well because the metal coins would reverberate when tossed into the containers. Many wealthy people put in large amounts, accompanied by loud clanging. But the poor widow puts in two small coins, creating two small pings. The word denotes the smallest coin in circulation at the time, an insignificant amount. The fact that she puts in two is significant because she could have chosen to keep one for herself. Yet, Jesus does not view her donation as insignificant. In fact he calls his disciples to witness her example, and he solemnly makes the point: "Truly I tell you, this poor widow has put in more than all those who are contributing to the treasury" (v. 43). The others were giving out of their surplus, whereas she gave out of her want, contributing all she had to live on. She illustrates the teaching of Jesus that commitment to God is expressed in wholehearted love, an offering that is "much more important than all whole burnt offerings and sacrifices" (12:33).

We can discover a further meaning to the contrast between the poor woman and the greedy scribes when we notice that the key word *widow* links both scenes. Because widows were some of the most vulnerable members of society, the Torah mandated special care for them, and the prophets denounced those who defrauded them. Jesus reproaches the scribes not only for their hypocrisy but especially because "they devour widows' houses" (v. 40). Though the precise practice to which Jesus is referring here is uncertain, the scribes in some way were using their status to exploit the widows for financial gain.

With this connection between the two scenes in mind, the action of the poor widow may be interpreted as an instance of the way the scribes prey upon the piety of the vulnerable widows to extort offerings from them far beyond what they can afford. The words of Jesus, in this sense, may be read as a lament of a religious system that takes advantage of the woman by prompting her to give her last cent. The fact that, in the verses immediately following this scene, Jesus predicts the destruction of the temple adds weight to this interpretation.

Though commentators often debate about whether the Gospel writer intended to praise the widow's action or deplore it, it seems that both meanings can be contained within the scene. Because the woman's total giving precedes the passion account, her action in the temple is a preview of Jesus's gift of his whole life. But because the widow's gift of her livelihood follows the condemnation of greedy temple officials and precedes the forecast of a crumbled temple, it seems that Jesus laments this woman's offering as the result of religious abuse. Like the sacrificial offering of Jesus on the cross, the woman's gift is both an injustice and a selfless offering. The scene is both lamentable and commendable, like the scene of crucifixion that will bring the Gospel to its climax.

After listening to the Gospel text with the ear of your heart, answer this questions about the Scriptures you have read:

‡ In what way can the gift of the widow be read as an overture to the passion of Jesus?

Meditatio

Place yourself within the scene and ponder its significance for the characters involved. Consider what you are learning from this scene in your continuing efforts to follow the way of Jesus more faithfully.

‡ Why was Jesus watching people putting their coins into the temple treasury? What was most noticed by the crowd? What did Jesus notice that others missed?

‡ What might Jesus see about me that others around me might miss? What does this teach me about my relationship with him?

‡ Why did Jesus point out the scene of the poor widow's offering to his disciples? What does Jesus want his church to understand from this episode?

Oratio

Offer your prayer to God in response to the scene of the poor widow. Express repentance or gratitude as directed by your heart and God's Spirit.

> Blessed are you, Lord God of Israel. You teach us that love of you and love of neighbor are more important than all the sacrifices and offerings in the temple. Teach me to open my heart to you and to give of myself generously and trustingly.

Continue to pray in your own words . . .

Contemplatio

Imagine that you are looking upon yourself with the eyes of God, with unconditional positive regard and indescribable love.

After your time of quiet, choose a few words that express the fruits of your silent contemplation.

Operatio

How can I avoid hypocritical religious practice? How can I make my discipleship more generous and uncalculating?

26

The Woman at Bethany Anoints Jesus

Lectio

Read this account aloud so that you can listen to this narrative of Jesus as he nears his passion. Try to imagine the scene as you read.

MARK 14:3–9

³While [Jesus] was at Bethany in the house of Simon the leper, as he sat at the table, a woman came with an alabaster jar of very costly ointment of nard, and she broke open the jar and poured the ointment on his head. ⁴But some were there who said to one another in anger, "Why was the ointment wasted in this way? ⁵For this ointment could have been sold for more than three hundred denarii, and the money given to the poor." And they scolded her. ⁶But Jesus said, "Let her alone; why do you trouble her? She has performed a good service for me. ⁷For you always have the poor with you, and you can show kindness to them whenever you wish; but you will not always have me. ⁸She has done what she could; she has anointed my body beforehand for its burial. ⁹Truly I tell you, wherever the good news is proclaimed in the whole world, what she has done will be told in remembrance of her."

After reading this account with your mind and heart engaged, search for further meaning through these comments.

In the midst of the dark treachery, greed, and betrayal of the passion account, this episode of the woman who anoints Jesus shines its warm glow. Like the poor widow at the temple, the woman at Bethany offers the disciples of Jesus a model of loving generosity. Her extravagant love foreshadows the unreserved giving that Jesus will demonstrate on the cross. Rather than opening the jar and carefully measuring out an appropriate amount, the woman breaks open the alabaster jar and lavishly pours out its entire contents upon the head of Jesus. We can imagine the smell of the aromatic perfume that fills the beautiful scene and briefly overcomes the stench of deceit and hostility that permeates the passion account.

The woman pours the oil on the head of Jesus, an action that has several levels of meaning. Banquet hosts often anointed the heads of their guests as an expression of hospitality and refreshment. The psalmist rejoices in God's blessings: "You prepare a table before me" and "You anoint my head with oil" (Ps. 23:5). On this level, the anointing is a gesture of kindness toward Jesus. On another level of meaning, the action expresses the recognition that Jesus is the Messiah. The kings of Israel were anointed with oil as a sign that God had chosen them, and the ideal descendant of David who was expected to restore God's people was called the Messiah, literally, "the anointed one." Even if the woman did not fully understand the meaning of her action, certainly the Gospel writer wanted his readers to note that the Messiah was anointed.

A further prophetic meaning of the woman's anointing is noted by Jesus: "She has anointed my body beforehand for its burial" (v. 8). Corpses were customarily anointed with perfumed oils before being placed in the tomb, and the woman offers the only anointing Jesus will receive. After his death, the body of Jesus will be placed in the tomb without the usual anointing because of the approach of the Sabbath. Through this anointing, the woman was giving what she could to Jesus, who was giving his life for her.

Nard oil was an expensive ointment that came from the roots of a rare Indian plant. The monetary worth of the oil, calculated as "more than three hundred denarii," was about a year's wages for an ordinary worker

(v. 5). Those who observed the scene thought that surely this oil could have been put to a more practical use in the form of alms for the poor. Yet, Jesus interrupts their scolding and defends her action: "She has performed a good service for me" (v. 6). Jesus's additional comment, "For you always have the poor with you" (v. 7) is not a justification for letting people live in poverty. His words allude to the Torah's directive to care for the needy: "Since there will never cease to be some in need on the earth, I therefore command you, 'Open your hand to the poor and needy neighbor in your land' " (Deut. 15:11).

Though God's people must always care for the needy, their opportunity to focus on Jesus is drawing to a close. Jesus concludes his defense of the woman with a majestic announcement: "Truly I tell you, wherever the good news is proclaimed in the whole world, what she has done will be told in remembrance of her" (v. 9). Because her action represents the loving and generous response of a disciple to the self-offering of Jesus, the proclamation of the gospel will be forever incomplete without the telling of this woman's deed. Jesus praised her deed more highly than he praised any other deed in the Gospel. Since the Good News of Jesus to the world is unfinished without discipleship, the woman at Bethany will forever be a model of the true and full response of discipleship to Jesus. The total gift of Jesus naturally draws forth an extravagant response.

After experiencing this scene and seeking its fullest meaning, test your understanding by answering these questions:

✢ What are the various levels of meaning in the woman's anointing of Jesus?

✢ Why does Jesus praise the woman at Bethany so profusely?

Meditatio

Allow the words of the scene to interact with your own world of ideas, concerns, thoughts, and feelings. Ask yourself what the text means to you.

✝ When was the last time I did something lavish and extravagant? Did the act express generosity and uncalculating love or did it communicate wasteful indulgence?

✝ If this woman's deed will forever be told "in memory of her," why is her name not remembered? Does her anonymity allow me to insert myself into the passion story more easily?

✝ Which words of the scene have the most impact on me? What does the woman at Bethany teach me about genuine discipleship?

Oratio

Speak to God in response to the words, ideas, and images of the Gospel text. Respond to the One who knows you intimately, cares about you deeply, and accepts you unconditionally.

Compassionate God, everything I have and everything I am is your gift to me. May I live my life as a grateful response to you, who have blessed me so abundantly. Give me a compassionate heart so that I will notice and respond generously to the needs of those around me.

Continue speaking to God in whatever ways seem to respond to the divine Word spoken to you . . .

Contemplatio

Try to contemplate the complete and total love of Jesus for you. Experience in quiet the fragrance of that love surrounding you.

Write a few words about your contemplative experience.

Operatio

What might be something beautiful and extravagant that I could do for Jesus in response to his total self-giving for me?

The Women of Jerusalem
Weep for Jesus

Lectio

*Listen to these thorny and challenging words of Jesus as he speaks to the
women of Jerusalem. Consider the words you find most difficult to hear and
understand.*

LUKE 23:26–31, 44–49

[26]As they led him away, they seized a man, Simon of Cyrene, who
was coming from the country, and they laid the cross on him, and
made him carry it behind Jesus. [27]A great number of the people followed him, and among them were women who were beating their
breasts and wailing for him. [28]But Jesus turned to them and said,
"Daughters of Jerusalem, do not weep for me, but weep for yourselves
and for your children. [29]For the days are surely coming when they
will say, 'Blessed are the barren, and the wombs that never bore, and
the breasts that never nursed.' [30]Then they will begin to say to the
mountains, 'Fall on us'; and to the hills, 'Cover us.' [31]For if they do
this when the wood is green, what will happen when it is dry?"

[44]It was now about noon, and darkness came over the whole land
until three in the afternoon, [45]while the sun's light failed; and the

curtain of the temple was torn in two. [46]Then Jesus, crying with a loud voice, said, "Father, into your hands I commend my spirit." Having said this, he breathed his last. [47]When the centurion saw what had taken place, he praised God and said, "Certainly this man was innocent." [48]And when all the crowds who had gathered there for this spectacle saw what had taken place, they returned home, beating their breasts. [49]But all his acquaintances, including the women who had followed him from Galilee, stood at a distance, watching these things.

Continue to listen to this Scripture from the passion account, seeking its full significance for the church.

Luke's passion account includes "a great number of people" who follow Jesus as he carries the cross to the place of his execution. Among them are "women who were beating their breasts and wailing for him" (v. 27). In Luke's usual attempt to include women as well as men in all the Gospel scenes, his Gospel alone adds these women of Jerusalem to the account of Simon of Cyrene. These local women are clearly devout and sympathetic toward Jesus in contrast to the people who abuse and mock him.

Jesus addresses the women as "daughters of Jerusalem" (v. 28), a phrase commonly found in the prophets, although usually in a positive sense: "Rejoice greatly, O daughter Zion! Shout aloud, O daughter Jerusalem!" (Zech. 9:9). Here the scene is one of deep grief and warning. Beating breasts and wailing are expressions of repentance and profound anguish.

This scene is sometimes wrongly entitled "Jesus consoles the women of Jerusalem," but the words of Jesus are clearly not a consolation. He speaks like a prophet of old and pronounces a judgment on the city. He urges the women not to lament for him but for themselves and their children (v. 28). Jesus had already warned about the Roman armies that would surround Jerusalem and brutally besiege and destroy the city. He had said, "Woe to those who are pregnant and to those who are nursing infants in those days!" (21:23).

The evil that has brought him to this dark hour will soon fall on the lives of all in Jerusalem. The suffering of those days will be so great that people will say, "Blessed are the barren, and the wombs that never bore, and the breasts that never nursed" (v. 29). It is a tragic beatitude. Instead of sterility being a curse, as it always was in the Hebrew Scriptures, it becomes a blessing. It is better not to have children and be spared seeing them suffer and die. The experience will be so dreadful that people will wish for death and burial to put an end to the horrors (v. 30).

Jesus's final mysterious statement to the women of Jerusalem compares his own suffering to "green wood" and the later suffering of Jerusalem to "dry wood" (v. 31). The prophet Ezekiel had warned the people that God would kindle a fire that "shall devour every green tree in you and every dry tree" (Ezek. 20:47). Jesus probably meant that if Jerusalem can put to death its innocent Messiah, who is like "green wood" not meant for the fire, how much more destruction is destined to fall upon this city, which is like "dry wood" ready for burning.

Luke's Gospel is also the only account to narrate the effects of the crucifixion and death of Jesus on the crowds in Jerusalem. He reports that the crowds who saw what had taken place "returned home, beating their breasts" (v. 48). In Luke, "beating the breasts" indicates contrition and repentance. The gesture adds a note of hope to the dark and tragic scene. Though suffering is inevitable for those who follow Jesus, the forgiveness and compassion of Jesus always have the last word.

After wrestling with this heartrending scene, seek to answer these questions:

‡ What indicates that Jesus is not offering consolation to the women of Jerusalem?

‡ What did Jesus mean in the tragic beatitude of verse 29?

Meditatio

Consider the message that Jesus is addressing to you in this passage from Luke's passion account.

✝ What are my greatest fears for my children or for the children of others?

✝ In times of violence and war, the innocent inevitably suffer along with the guilty. Why do such times affect women and children most severely?

✝ Knowing that suffering will be an inevitable part of their lives, is it worth bringing children into the world?

Oratio

Respond in prayer to Jesus's warning to the women and to his tragic crucifixion. Bring to God your fears and your hopes.

Creator God, you give us the privilege of nurturing children and fostering your life within them. Help me to love the children of our world and to give them hope for your reign over creation.

Continue to pray in response to the Word you have heard . . .

Contemplatio

Relax in the assurance that you are a son of Abraham, a daughter of Jerusalem. Know that you are specially chosen and beloved of God. Trust in the God who forms you as his family.

Write a few words that linger from your silent time in God's presence.

Operatio

How is God relieving my fears through my lectio divina? What can I do to help relieve the fears of others?

28

Galilean Women at the Cross and at the Tomb

Lectio

Read these accounts of the followers of Jesus who were faithful to the end. Speak the names of these women with loving reverence for their affectionate devotion to Jesus.

MARK 15:40–41, 47

⁴⁰There were also women looking on from a distance; among them were Mary Magdalene, and Mary the mother of James the younger and of Joses, and Salome. ⁴¹These used to follow him and provided for him when he was in Galilee; and there were many other women who had come up with him to Jerusalem.

⁴⁷Mary Magdalene and Mary the mother of Joses saw where the body was laid.

MATTHEW 27:55–56, 61

⁵⁵Many women were also there, looking on from a distance; they had followed Jesus from Galilee and had provided for him. ⁵⁶Among them were Mary Magdalene, and Mary the mother of James and Joseph, and the mother of the sons of Zebedee.

⁶¹Mary Magdalene and the other Mary were there, sitting opposite the tomb.

LUKE 23:49, 55–56

⁴⁹But all his acquaintances, including the women who had followed him from Galilee, stood at a distance, watching these things.

⁵⁵The women who had come with him from Galilee followed, and they saw the tomb and how his body was laid. ⁵⁶Then they returned, and prepared spices and ointments. On the sabbath they rested according to the commandment.

JOHN 19:25–27

²⁵Meanwhile, standing near the cross of Jesus were his mother, and his mother's sister, Mary the wife of Clopas, and Mary Magdalene. ²⁶When Jesus saw his mother and the disciple whom he loved standing beside her, he said to his mother, "Woman, here is your son." ²⁷Then he said to the disciple, "Here is your mother." And from that hour the disciple took her into his own home.

After listening with devotion to these inspired texts, continue seeking their fuller meaning and significance for communities of faith.

All four of the Gospels mention a group of women who were looking on as Jesus was crucified. These women had been with Jesus from his ministry in Galilee and had remained with him until the end. The verbs used to describe the actions of these women indicate that they are true disciples. Mark's Gospel says they used to "follow" Jesus in Galilee, a word indicating discipleship. It also states that the women "provided" for him, a word that can also mean "served" or "ministered," another indication of genuine discipleship. And finally, Mark states that these women "had come up with him to Jerusalem," referring to their unity with him in the fulfillment of his mission in the way of the cross. Their faithful following and service are models for all future disciples.

Though each Gospel mentions only a few women by name, both Matthew and Mark state that there were many more women who had come with Jesus from Galilee. It is possible that Jesus had as many female disciples as male disciples who followed him along the way. The freedom that these women enjoyed, traveling with an itinerant band of disciples, must have seemed extraordinary and attracted attention in the culture of the times.

The Gospel writers found it important to note that these women were at the cross of Jesus. The Synoptic Gospels state that they were looking on "from a distance" during his crucifixion and death. They were far enough away from the cross so as not to give active assent to what was happening but close enough to be sympathetic witnesses to these climactic events. Their presence during Jesus's dark hours is a stark reminder of the flight of the chosen "twelve" at the arrest of Jesus and their glaring absence at the cross. John's Gospel says that the women were "standing near the cross of Jesus" (v. 25), probably an indication of emotional closeness as well as spatial nearness.

Each of the Gospel writers mentions a few women by name as disciples of Jesus. Though it is tempting to suppose that the women are the same but designated differently in each Gospel, it is probably best to presume that these are all different women. For example, "Salome" of Mark's account is probably not "the mother of the sons of Zebedee" in Matthew's version, and "Mary the mother of James and Joseph" in Matthew is probably not "Mary the wife of Clopas" in John's account. Since "many women" followed Jesus from Galilee, each writer chose those women who were the most significant for the community addressed by his own Gospel.

These women form an important link between the Galilean ministry of Jesus and the paschal events of his passion, death, and resurrection. As consistent witnesses, they affirm the continuity of his mission, from the beginning until its glorious completion. They must have been bewildered and heartbroken to watch as Jesus died on the cross. The One who proclaimed the Good News, the One in whom they had learned to place their trust, had been executed in the most humiliating way. Yet, love clings to Christ, even when the mind cannot understand, and the women were unable to leave him.

Meditatio

Ponder the scenes of the faithful women at the cross and consider how they might deepen your own discipleship.

✝ When my discipleship is tested, do I stand at the cross, look on from a distance, or flee from the scene?

✝ How do the Gospel writers contrast these women of Galilee with the twelve male disciples of Jesus? How do the women demonstrate the most important characteristics of discipleship?

✝ Why is it significant that the women saw where the body of Jesus was laid in the tomb? What do the women at the cross of Jesus teach me about fidelity?

Oratio

Having listened and reflected on God's Word to you in the Gospel text, now respond to God from your heart in prayer.

> Merciful Jesus, your crucifixion expresses your supreme love for your disciples. Help me to faithfully follow and serve you in the way of the cross. Teach me to imitate the women from Galilee and to witness your life, death, and resurrection.

Continue praying in whatever words seem to express the content of your heart . . .

Contemplatio

Imaginatively place yourself at the cross of Jesus. Allow yourself to experience the grief, devotion, love, gratitude, or whatever emotion fills your heart during your time of silence.

What words come to mind after your contemplative time in God's presence?

Operatio

What difference does it make to me that I follow a crucified Messiah? How does the cross of Jesus affect the way I live my life?

29

The Women of Galilee
Proclaim the Resurrection

Lectio

Read aloud the resurrection accounts, imagining the experiences of the women at the tomb. Mark the phrases in each account that stand out to you.

MARK 16:1–8

[1]When the sabbath was over, Mary Magdalene, and Mary the mother of James, and Salome bought spices, so that they might go and anoint him. [2]And very early on the first day of the week, when the sun had risen, they went to the tomb. [3]They had been saying to one another, "Who will roll away the stone for us from the entrance to the tomb?" [4]When they looked up, they saw that the stone, which was very large, had already been rolled back. [5]As they entered the tomb, they saw a young man, dressed in a white robe, sitting on the right side; and they were alarmed. [6]But he said to them, "Do not be alarmed; you are looking for Jesus of Nazareth, who was crucified. He has been raised; he is not here. Look, there is the place they laid him. [7]But go, tell his disciples and Peter that he is going ahead of you to Galilee; there you will see him, just as he told you." [8]So they went out and fled from the tomb, for terror and amazement had seized them; and they said nothing to anyone, for they were afraid.

¹After the sabbath, as the first day of the week was dawning, Mary Magdalene and the other Mary went to see the tomb. ²And suddenly there was a great earthquake; for an angel of the Lord, descending from heaven, came and rolled back the stone and sat on it. ³His appearance was like lightning, and his clothing white as snow. ⁴For fear of him the guards shook and became like dead men. ⁵But the angel said to the women, "Do not be afraid; I know that you are looking for Jesus who was crucified. ⁶He is not here; for he has been raised, as he said. Come, see the place where he lay. ⁷Then go quickly and tell his disciples, 'He has been raised from the dead, and indeed he is going ahead of you to Galilee; there you will see him.' This is my message for you." ⁸So they left the tomb quickly with fear and great joy, and ran to tell his disciples. ⁹Suddenly Jesus met them and said, "Greetings!" And they came to him, took hold of his feet, and worshiped him. ¹⁰Then Jesus said to them, "Do not be afraid; go and tell my brothers to go to Galilee; there they will see me."

LUKE 24:1–12

¹But on the first day of the week, at early dawn, they came to the tomb, taking the spices that they had prepared. ²They found the stone rolled away from the tomb, ³but when they went in, they did not find the body. ⁴While they were perplexed about this, suddenly two men in dazzling clothes stood beside them. ⁵The women were terrified and bowed their faces to the ground, but the men said to them, "Why do you look for the living among the dead? He is not here, but has risen. ⁶Remember how he told you, while he was still in Galilee, ⁷that the Son of Man must be handed over to sinners, and be crucified, and on the third day rise again." ⁸Then they remembered his words, ⁹and returning from the tomb, they told all this to the eleven and to all the rest. ¹⁰Now it was Mary Magdalene, Joanna, Mary the mother of James, and the other women with them who told this to the apostles. ¹¹But these words seemed to them an idle tale, and they did not believe them. ¹²But Peter got up and ran to the tomb; stooping and looking in, he saw the linen cloths by themselves; then he went home, amazed at what had happened.

Following your careful listening to these resurrection narratives, continue seeking their fullest meaning for the church.

The women disciples, according to the resurrection accounts of the Gospels, are the first people to find the tomb of Jesus empty. Furthermore, they are the only witnesses to the empty tomb who had seen Jesus buried and so could testify it was really the tomb in which the body of Jesus had been laid. Just as these women formed the link between Jesus's ministry in Galilee and his passion and death in Jerusalem, they now create the critical connection between the burial of Jesus and his resurrection.

The fact that women were generally perceived to be unreliable witnesses in the ancient world points to the historical nature of these accounts. If the Gospel writers had wanted to fabricate a legend about Jesus risen from the tomb, they certainly would not have used the testimony of women. Yet, according to all the Gospels, it was indeed a handful of women who first delivered the Good News to the world that Jesus had risen from the dead. By reversing the usual and expected priority of men over women, the resurrection accounts rule out gender privilege and discrimination in the new world order begun with the resurrection.

Each Gospel writer has his own distinctive emphasis in telling the resurrection narrative. In Mark's Gospel, the messenger commissions the women to go and tell the disciples that Jesus is going ahead of them to Galilee, where they will see him. In this revelation lies the promise of forgiveness and a new beginning for those who denied and deserted him. The Gospel then ends abruptly, according to all the earliest texts of Mark, as the women flee from the tomb in terror and amazement. Though later editors added endings to the Gospel that seemed more complete, Mark's purpose was to leave the Gospel open-ended. Writing to teach people in the generation after Jesus how to be disciples, Mark wanted to show that the resurrection of Jesus is not the end of the story but only a new beginning. It is up to each individual in every generation to come to know and experience the risen Jesus.

Matthew's account demonstrates the cosmic implications of Jesus's resurrection by emphasizing the earthquake and the descending angel, who rolls back the stone for the women to see the empty tomb. As the women are rushing from the tomb to tell the news, the risen Jesus meets them. Though they prostrate themselves and clasp his feet, Jesus does not allow the women to linger in adoration. Instead, he encourages them to go fearlessly on their mission of proclaiming the Good News.

In Luke's narrative of the empty tomb, the two divine messengers ask the women, "Why do you look for the living among the dead?" (v. 5). The question challenges the women to take up their new mission as proclaimers of the Good News. The messengers remind the women, and the women remember, that Jesus had told them of his coming passion, death, and resurrection while still in Galilee. The reminder confirms that the women were among the disciples to whom Jesus shared his most intimate revelations during his ministry. Luke's Gospel ending prepares for the beginning of his second volume, the Acts of the apostles, the account of men and women ministering together in the early church.

After listening to these resurrection accounts, seek the answers to the following questions:

✝ What is Mark trying to communicate to the reader with the abrupt ending to his Gospel?

✝ Which names of the women are the same in each account and which are different in the Gospels of Mark, Matthew, and Luke? Why are there different names in each account?

Meditatio

Reflect on the reality that you are called to continue the mission of the women that began at the empty tomb. Ask yourself what you can learn from them.

‡ How does the fact that women were the first to witness the empty tomb point to the historical nature of these accounts? What helps me believe in Christ's resurrection?

‡ How does each Gospel describe the emotional response of the women at the discovery that Jesus has risen? In what ways do these emotions seem genuine?

‡ What was the significance to the early church that women were the first witnesses to Christ's resurrection? What is its message to me?

Oratio

Pray for the courage and zeal to continue the mission of the women to proclaim the news of resurrection through the life you live.

Glorious God, you raised Jesus from the dead through your mighty power and defeated all the forces that could hold us in the bondage of fear and futility. Instill within me a tremendous awe at the wondrous act of Christ and help me to witness the resurrection in word and action.

Continue to pray as the Holy Spirit prompts you . . .

Contemplatio

When words are no longer necessary or helpful in your prayer, just remain in quiet to appreciate the presence of the risen Christ within you. Know that God is working within you through your openness to Christ's divine presence.

Write a few words to describe your time of contemplatio.

Operatio

Think about how to be a more effective witness of Christ's resurrection in the world. How can I be a sign of Christ today in what I say and do?

30

Mary Magdalene
Announces the Good News

Lectio

Ask the Holy Spirit to open your eyes, ears, lips, and heart as the inspired text proclaims Mary Magdalene's experience of Christ's resurrection.

JOHN 20:1–18

[1] Early on the first day of the week, while it was still dark, Mary Magdalene came to the tomb and saw that the stone had been removed from the tomb. [2] So she ran and went to Simon Peter and the other disciple, the one whom Jesus loved, and said to them, "They have taken the Lord out of the tomb, and we do not know where they have laid him." [3] Then Peter and the other disciple set out and went toward the tomb. [4] The two were running together, but the other disciple outran Peter and reached the tomb first. [5] He bent down to look in and saw the linen wrappings lying there, but he did not go in. [6] Then Simon Peter came, following him, and went into the tomb. He saw the linen wrappings lying there, [7] and the cloth that had been on Jesus' head, not lying with the linen wrappings but rolled up in a place by itself. [8] Then the other disciple, who reached the tomb

first, also went in, and he saw and believed; ⁹for as yet they did not understand the scripture, that he must rise from the dead. ¹⁰Then the disciples returned to their homes.

¹¹But Mary stood weeping outside the tomb. As she wept, she bent over to look into the tomb; ¹²and she saw two angels in white, sitting where the body of Jesus had been lying, one at the head and the other at the feet. ¹³They said to her, "Woman, why are you weeping?" She said to them, "They have taken away my Lord, and I do not know where they have laid him." ¹⁴When she had said this, she turned around and saw Jesus standing there, but she did not know that it was Jesus. ¹⁵Jesus said to her, "Woman, why are you weeping? Whom are you looking for?" Supposing him to be the gardener, she said to him, "Sir, if you have carried him away, tell me where you have laid him, and I will take him away." ¹⁶Jesus said to her, "Mary!" She turned and said to him in Hebrew, "Rabbouni!" (which means Teacher). ¹⁷Jesus said to her, "Do not hold on to me, because I have not yet ascended to the Father. But go to my brothers and say to them, 'I am ascending to my Father and your Father, to my God and your God.'" ¹⁸Mary Magdalene went and announced to the disciples, "I have seen the Lord"; and she told them that he had said these things to her.

After listening to the inspired text, read this commentary to continue your search for meaning.

Mary of Magdala is the only woman described in all four Gospels as a witness both at the cross and at the resurrection. In John's Gospel, Mary Magdalene comes alone to the tomb in the morning darkness of the week's first day. On the first of her two visits to the tomb, she sees that the stone has been moved from the tomb's entrance. Her only possible conclusion in her pre-resurrection world is grave robbing: "They have taken the Lord out of the tomb" (vv. 2, 13). Mary runs to tell Peter and the beloved disciple, the anonymous model disciple of the Gospel, and the two then race to the tomb. Peter enters the tomb first, and the beloved disciple is the first to believe, but Mary Magdalene models the ideal response to the risen Lord as she encounters him in the garden.

While Peter and the beloved disciple return to their homes, Mary remains vigilant at the tomb. As a woman who dearly loves Jesus, Mary is overwhelmed with her loss and cries tears of grief (vv. 11, 13, 15). When Jesus asks her why she is weeping and for whom she is looking, she sees him but does not realize it is Jesus. Only when he calls her by name, "Mary," does she recognize Jesus (v. 16). The calling of her name enables Mary to give Jesus her full attention and to create the personal bond with him that establishes belief.

Knowing that Jesus is risen, she instinctively embraces him. But Jesus gently asks her not to "hold on" to him because he has not yet returned to the Father (v. 17). She is trying to hold on to Jesus as if he were still in the flesh. Mary and the other disciples must learn a new way of knowing Jesus. His permanent presence with them will come only with the gift of the Spirit as he ascends to the Father.

Mary Magdalene becomes the first to announce the Good News of Jesus's resurrection to others. When she proclaims, "I have seen the Lord" (v. 18), she is referring to an experience far deeper and more real than simply a visual sighting. The experience is one of loving recognition, a deeply personal and mystical encounter. Mary has moved from the darkness to the light of faith. She has seen Jesus as Lord, and she cannot help but become the messenger of that Good News to others.

Because Mary Magdalene was the premiere witness to the resurrection and, at the command of Jesus, the first to announce the gospel of the risen Lord to the others, the early church rightly bestowed upon her the title of apostle to the apostles. Her announcement, "I have seen the Lord," is the same credential used by Paul to insist on his own authority as an apostle: "Am I not an apostle? Have I not seen Jesus our Lord?" (1 Cor. 9:1). The church's belief in the resurrection originated with the evangelical witness of this woman. Her testimony was accepted and believed not only by the original disciples but also by the universal church, which collectively remembers her witness as the foundation of apostolic faith in Christ's resurrection.

Meditatio

Enlightened by Mary Magdalene's faith in the risen Christ, consider your own understanding of resurrection and its implications for your life.

✝ What is the meaning of Mary Magdalene's proclamation, "I have seen the Lord"?

✝ What strikes me most about the encounter between Jesus and Mary Magdalene at the empty tomb?

✝ Why is Mary Magdalene called the apostle to the apostles? How is Mary Magdalene a model of faith for me?

Oratio

Respond in prayer to God's Word spoken to you through this resurrection narrative.

> Risen Lord, you are the beginning of God's new creation, the light that shines in the world's darkness. Turn my weeping to joy, my despair to hope, and my disbelief to the fullness of confident trust.

Continue to respond with confident trust in the Lord who calls you to proclaim the Good News you have heard to others . . .

Contemplatio

Entrust your heart to the One who scatters the darkness and lives in triumph forever. Ask the risen Lord to give you peace.

Write a few words to conclude your time of peaceful contemplation.

Operatio

How has this study of the women of the Gospels shaped and changed me? What do I most want to remember and incorporate into my life?

Ancient-Future Bible Study for Small Groups

A small group for *collatio*, the communal practice of lectio divina, is a wonderful way to let the power of Scripture more deeply nourish participants. Through the thoughts, reflections, prayers, and experiences of the other members of the group, each individual comes to understand Scripture more intensely and experience it more profoundly. By sharing our understanding and wisdom in a faith-filled group of people, we discover how to let God live in every dimension of our lives and we enrich the lives of others.

These groups may be formed in any number of ways, just as you create groups for other learning experiences within your community. Groups composed of no more than a dozen people are best for this experience. It is preferable to give people with various needs a variety of days and times from which to choose.

Small groups are best formed when people are encouraged and supported by a church's pastoral leadership and personally welcomed into these small communities. Personally directed invitations are most effective for convincing people to add another dimension to their schedules.

The collatio should never take the place of one's regular, personal lectio divina. Rather, a weekly communal practice is an ideal extension and continuation of personal, daily sacred reading. At each group session, participants discuss the fruits of their individual lectio divina and practice elements of lectio divina together.

Participants should read carefully the opening sections of this book before joining the group. "The Movements of Lectio Divina," "The Essence of Lectio Divina," and "Your Personal Practice of Ancient-Future Bible Study" would be helpful sections to review throughout the course of the study.

The full weekly collatio group session is designed for about ninety minutes. Those groups with limited time may choose either Part 1 or Part 2 for the group experience. Instructions for each of the collatio groups are provided on the following pages.

Suggestions for
Participating in the Group

‡ The spirit of the collatio should be that of a personal conversation, with the members desiring to learn from one another and building each other up. The divine Word is the teacher; the members of the group are all learners.

‡ The group can avoid the distraction of off-topic chatter by sticking to the text, the commentary, and their personal response to the text from the meditatio.

‡ Group members should be careful to give everyone in the group an opportunity to share. When discussing personal thoughts, members should use "I" language and be cautious about giving advice to others. They should listen attentively to the other members of the group so as to learn from their insights and should not worry about trying to cover all the questions in each gathering. They should select only those that seem the most helpful for group discussion.

‡ Dispute, debate, and dogmatic hairsplitting within the group erode its focus and purpose. Opposition and division destroy the supportive bond of the group. The desire of individuals to assert themselves and their own ideas wears down the spirit of the group. In a community setting, it is often wise to "agree to disagree." An inflexible, pedantic attitude blocks the way to a vital and fulfilling understanding of the passage. The Scriptures are the living Word of God, the full meaning of which we can never exhaust.

‡ It is usually helpful to have someone to guide the process of the group. This facilitator directs the discussion, helping the group keep the discussion on time and on track. The facilitator need not be an expert, either in Scripture or in the process of lectio divina, but simply a person with the skills necessary to guide a group. This role may be rotated among members of the group, if desired.

Group Study in Six Sessions

‡ Begin each group session with hospitality and welcome. Name tags are helpful if group members don't know one another. Offer any announcements or instructions before entering the spirit of prayer.

‡ Set the tone and focus the group by saying the gathering prayer together.

‡ Note that the first group session is a bit different from the others because it involves reading and discussing the introduction to this book. After the first group session, all the remaining sessions follow the same format.

‡ The group sessions are in two parts. Part 1 is a discussion of the fruits of the lectio divina that participants completed on their own since the last group session. The most effective question you can ask of each chapter is this: "What insight is most significant to you from your reflection on this chapter?" Group members may mention insights they gained in the lectio, meditatio, oratio, contemplatio, or operatio of each chapter.

‡ Part 2 is a session of lectio divina in the group. Leave at least half of the group time for this section. Move through each of the five movements as described in the chapter. Read the text aloud, followed by the commentary. Leave the most time for the more personal questions of the meditatio. Don't worry if you don't complete them all.

‡ Leave sufficient time for the oratio, contemplatio, and operatio. These movements should not be rushed. Gently guide the group from vocal prayer into a period of restful silence. Don't neglect to conclude the lectio divina by mentioning some practical fruits of operatio before dismissing the group into the world of daily discipleship.

‡ Conclude each group session by encouraging participants to complete the lectio divina on their own for the upcoming chapters. Ask them to write their responses to each movement of lectio in their book.

Collatio Group 1

‡ The first group session is a bit different from the others. After offering greetings and introductions, explain the process of Ancient-Future Bible Study. Then set the tone for the group experience by praying together the gathering prayer.

‡ Gathering prayer:

> *Come upon us, Holy Spirit, to enlighten and guide us as we begin this study of* Women of the Gospels: Friends and Disciples of Jesus. *You have inspired the Gospel writers to give to your church a living Word that has the power to convert our hearts and change our lives. Give us a sense of expectation, trusting that you will shine the light of your truth within us. Bless us as we gather with your gifts of wisdom and discernment so that we may listen to the inspired Word and experience its transforming energy.*

‡ Spend the first half of the collatio group reading the introduction to this book and discussing the questions to consider. A volunteer may read each section aloud, and the group will spend a few minutes discussing the questions that follow.

‡ Spend the second half of the group time following the five movements of the lectio divina at the end of the introduction. Read the text aloud, followed by the commentary. Then spend time reflecting and sharing responses to the questions of the meditatio.

‡ When leading into the oratio, pray the prayer aloud, then leave time for additional prayers from the group. When the vocal prayer has receded, lead the group into contemplatio. Help the group to feel comfortable with the quiet and relax in the presence of God. Conclude the lectio divina with the operatio. Share encouragement and commitment to practice lectio divina throughout the week.

‡ Before departing, instruct group members in their practice of lectio divina during the week. Participants should complete the lectio divina for chapters 1–5 for next week. Encourage them to write their responses to each movement of lectio in their book. The lectio divina for chapter 6 will be done together in the group next week.

Collatio Group 2

✠ Gathering prayer:

> *Creating and redeeming God, the history of your people Israel is filled with female heroes, prophets, and wisdom figures through whom you prepared the world for the coming of Christ. In the infancy narratives of Jesus, your Word prepares our hearts through Elizabeth, the barren wife; Mary, the young maiden; and Anna, the elderly prophet. May these models of patience, trust, and devotion deepen our desire to receive Jesus and give us a passionate desire for your Word.*

✠ Part 1:
- Having completed the lectio divina for chapters 1–5 during the week, the group members discuss the fruit of their practice for these five chapters. Divide these chapters into equal time allotments so that no chapter is neglected. To provoke personal discussion of each chapter, ask this question: "What insight is most significant to you from your reflection on this chapter?"

✠ Part 2:
- Spend at least the last half of the group time in the full lectio divina of chapter 6. Move through each step according to the instructions provided in the chapter, leaving plenty of time for oratio, contemplatio, and operatio.

✠ Departure:
- Encourage participants to complete the lectio divina for chapters 7–11 before the next collatio group. Ask them to write their responses to each movement of lectio in their book. The lectio divina for chapter 12 will be done together in the group next week.

Collatio Group 3

✠ Gathering prayer:

> *Compassionate God, the saving presence of Jesus brought healing and wholeness to the suffering women of the Gospels. As you extended mercy to your daughters, they rose in gratitude to praise you and serve your people. Teach us to be instruments of*

your compassionate healing to the people of our world through the study of these Scriptures. Give us a deep desire to understand, accept, and live your Word as disciples of Jesus your Son.

✝ Part 1:
- Having completed the lectio divina for chapters 7–11 during the week, the group members discuss the fruit of their practice for these five chapters. Divide these chapters into equal time allotments so that no chapter is neglected. To provoke personal discussion of each chapter, ask this question: "What insight is most significant to you from your reflection on this chapter?"

✝ Part 2:
- Spend at least the last half of the group time in the full lectio divina of chapter 12. Move through each step according to the instructions provided in the chapter, leaving plenty of time for oratio, contemplatio, and operatio.

✝ Departure:
- Encourage participants to complete the lectio divina for chapters 13–17 before the next collatio group. Ask them to write their responses to each movement of lectio in their book. The lectio divina for chapter 18 will be done together in the group next week.

Collatio Group 4

✝ Gathering prayer:

> *God of freedom and life, in the Gospel of Luke we are inspired by the stories of wise, brave, and generous women who stand side by side with men in your new community. We are grateful for this community of faith in which we are gathered and for all those who help us understand your Word and live in Christ. Help us to see the needs of others as Jesus sees them, to hear the cries of those in need with his merciful heart.*

✝ Part 1:
- Having completed the lectio divina for chapters 13–17 during the week, the group members discuss the fruit of their practice for these five chapters. Divide these chapters into equal time allotments so that no

chapter is neglected. To provoke personal discussion of each chapter, ask this question: "What insight is most significant to you from your reflection on this chapter?"

‡ Part 2:
- Spend at least the last half of the group time in the full lectio divina of chapter 18. Move through each step according to the instructions provided in the chapter, leaving plenty of time for oratio, contemplatio, and operatio.

‡ Departure:
- Encourage participants to complete the lectio divina for chapters 19–23 before the next collatio group. Ask them to write their responses to each movement of lectio in their book. The lectio divina for chapter 24 will be done together in the group next week.

Collatio Group 5

‡ Gathering prayer:

> *Lord our God, in the Gospel of John you give us the examples of Mary of Nazareth, the woman of Samaria, Martha and Mary of Bethany, and Mary of Magdala to be our inspiration in the way of discipleship and witness to Jesus. Through the guidance of these great women of faith, help us understand our faith and teach us to follow your Son in the way of discipleship. May we witness to our faith by living faithfully in your grace.*

‡ Part 1:
- Having completed the lectio divina for chapters 19–23 during the week, the group members discuss the fruit of their practice for these five chapters. Divide these chapters into equal time allotments so that no chapter is neglected. The most effective question to ask of each chapter is this: "What is your most important insight from this chapter?"

‡ Part 2:
- Spend at least the last half of the group time in the full lectio divina of chapter 24. Move through each step according to the instructions provided in the chapter, leaving plenty of time for oratio, contemplatio, and operatio.

‡ Departure:
  • Encourage participants to complete the lectio divina for chapters 25–29 before the next collatio group. Ask them to write their responses to each movement of lectio in their book. The lectio divina for chapter 30 will be done together in the group next week.

Collatio Group 6
‡ Gathering prayer:

> *Merciful God, the women of the passion accounts offer us models of faithful discipleship in the midst of trial and suffering. By remaining at the cross and the tomb of Jesus, they became the first witnesses to his resurrection. May these friends of Jesus become truly our sisters in Christ. Give us courage in our struggles and steadiness in our discipleship. Bless us as we gather in the name of Jesus and make us witnesses of his risen life in our world.*

‡ Part 1:
  • Having completed the lectio divina for chapters 25–29 during the week, the group members discuss the fruit of their practice for these five chapters. Divide these chapters into equal time allotments so that no chapter is neglected. The most effective question to ask of each chapter is this: "What is your most important insight from this chapter?"

‡ Part 2:
  • Spend at least the last half of the group time in the full lectio divina of chapter 30. Move through each step according to the instructions provided in the chapter, leaving plenty of time for oratio, contemplatio, and operatio.

‡ Departure:
  • Discuss how this Ancient-Future Bible Study has made a difference in the lives of group members and whether the group wishes to study another book in the series. Consult www.brazospress.com/ancient futurebiblestudy for more study options.